THE DEATH
OF THE
SALESMAN
AND THE
RISE
OF THE
TRUSTED FINANCIAL
ADVISOR

ANDRE ROOS

authorHOUSE

AuthorHouse™ UK
1663 Liberty Drive
Bloomington, IN 47403 USA
www.authorhouse.co.uk
Phone: 0800.197.4150

© 2018 Andre Roos. All rights reserved.

No part of this book may be reproduced, stored in a retrieval system, or transmitted by any means without the written permission of the author.

Published by AuthorHouse 06/18/2018

ISBN: 978-1-5462-8865-7 (sc)
ISBN: 978-1-5462-8866-4 (hc)
ISBN: 978-1-5462-8864-0 (e)

Print information available on the last page.

Any people depicted in stock imagery provided by Getty Images are models, and such images are being used for illustrative purposes only.
Certain stock imagery © Getty Images.

This book is printed on acid-free paper.

Because of the dynamic nature of the Internet, any web addresses or links contained in this book may have changed since publication and may no longer be valid. The views expressed in this work are solely those of the author and do not necessarily reflect the views of the publisher, and the publisher hereby disclaims any responsibility for them.

I dedicate this book to my dear friend, the late Gregory Leonard Basson, who recruited me into the wonderful world of financial services. He saw my potential well before I could see it myself, put up with my endless questions, and was always ready, willing, and able to guide me through whatever challenges I faced. May your legacy live on.

CONTENTS

Preface ix
Introduction xi

Chapter 1   Snake Oil—Are You Selling It?............................... 1
Chapter 2   The Roseto Effect... 13
Chapter 3   Effective Sales Suicide Techniques 24
Chapter 4   Sales Courtesy 32
Chapter 5   "The Formula" 42
Chapter 6   The Five Professionals 58
Chapter 7   Nurture Your Investment..................................... 66
Chapter 8   Jack of All Trades, Master of None 77
Chapter 9   Judge a Book by Its Profile 85
Chapter 10 The Prophet of Doom 93
Chapter 11 Taming the Future Dragon.................................103
Chapter 12 Barriers, Boundaries, Balls, and Walls.................111

Notes 121

PREFACE

If you've ever worked in any type of sales capacity, it is likely that you participated in some form of training prior to getting started. Through such training, it's possible that you learned how to watch for buying signals, how to mimic behaviour, how to influence your prospect to take certain actions, and—when the time is just right—how to move in for the close.

It is also probable that, if your experience is like that of more than 90 per cent of other sales professionals around the world, these tactics failed miserably.

Why?

Because today's consumer, regardless of what they are purchasing, is much more adept at deciphering when they are being "sold." And nobody ever likes to feel like they've been sold.

Buyers now, whether they are purchasing for business or personal reasons, would much rather be educated on potential scenarios and then come to a decision themselves on the solution that fits their specific needs the best. This is particularly the case when working with intangible offerings like insurance and financial strategies.

Gone are the days of the one-size-fits-all product. Thankfully, too, the snake oil salesmen of the past are now only a distant memory. That being the case, though, why are the majority of sales training programs still using these outdated tactics today?

One reason is simply that most organizations continue to use what they've had in place for many years. Doing so, however, can result in fewer sales, an unmotivated group of representatives, and customers who end up buying from someplace else. That "someplace else" in financial services is typically via a trusted advisor.

If you want to be the trusted advisor whom clients and prospects turn to, it will require that you take a very different approach—and that begins with having a different mindset.

In order to be successful in sales, you don't need to coerce people into buying, you don't need to use reverse psychology, and you don't need an endless list of clients. In fact, you don't even need "sales" skills at all.

But you do need to be viewed as a trusted advisor. In order to get to that level, you need a tried and true system that you can easily follow to get you from where you are right now to where you want to be.

That system is exactly what you'll find in this book.

INTRODUCTION

Your success as a leader will always be based on the degree to which you are trusted by your stakeholders.

—Unknown

Have you ever observed the top performers in your organization? Typically, these individuals aren't frazzled, even though they have plenty of new and existing clients to keep them busy. Nor do they appear to be following a sales script that was designed to lead them to the close.

Rather, these top performers, for the most part, seem to operate in a calm and confident manner. They almost effortlessly earn the business of each and every person they meet.

How do they achieve this elite status, along with the respect of their clients and co-workers, while others who have the exact same products and services to offer fall flat?

A large part of their success comes from attaining and maintaining the status of a trusted advisor. Yet nobody is simply born with such status. By having the proper road map in hand, and then following where it leads, anyone can learn to be a trusted advisor. That road map is the book you are now holding in your hands.

Who Needs This Book?

Just as the needs of each client differ, so do the ways in which an insurance or financial advisor will interact with them. If, however, you want to be viewed as a truly trusted advisor in the eyes of those you serve, you must still follow a specific framework.

Here in this guide, you will find answers to questions regarding how to establish trust, how to alter your status from "salesperson" to valued consultant, and how to build upon your success in order to run a thriving organization.

Just some of what you will learn here includes:

- how and why *not* to pitch your product
- why selling to anybody who has a pulse isn't a viable business-building strategy
- where to find the fine line between being informative and being too enthusiastic about your product or service offerings
- why scare tactics and urgency no longer work for closing sales with clients (at least not if you want to be viewed as a trusted advisor)
- how using a scripted approach can create *sales suicide*—and what you need to do instead
- how to decipher who fits into your one-third category
- how to keep your business, your clients, and yourself happy and healthy
- where and when to leave your digital footprints, and when to cover them up or erase them completely
- why clients will respect you, even when you tell them things that they don't necessarily want to hear
- why working with other professionals is a win-win scenario for everyone
- how to nurture client relationships once they're established
- why being well-rounded can actually hinder your progress
- how you can establish the right formula that can literally guarantee your success

For those who want to get off of the proverbial sales process treadmill, this book is a must. The information herein will provide you with a solid foundation for building your trusted advisory practice. It includes strategies, tips, and best practices that can lead you to both sales and success. It will also give you a running head start by providing valuable action steps that you can take.

How to Accomplish the Most with the Information You Will Learn

Although knowledge may be power, knowledge without action is useless. Within the pages of this guide, you will find information and resources, as well as actionable items that help you to immediately implement what you have learned. This can help you to more easily lock in the concepts and to engage the momentum that is needed for making positive, profitable changes in yourself and in your business.

Each chapter offers specific information on how and why the sales techniques of the past no longer work, and how you can replace these outdated tactics with methods of securing clients who want to work with you for the long term.

By closely following the processes that you will discover in this book, you can say goodbye to gambling on endless cold calls, and instead draw in those valued clients with whom you most want to work.

In addition, you will be able to pare down your list of clients in order to spend the bulk of your time with those who best fit with your business model. The others can be passed along to more fitting advisors for their particular needs—yet another win-win scenario for all involved.

So, if you're ready to become the trusted advisor that you always knew you could be, turn the page and let's get started!

CHAPTER 1

SNAKE OIL—ARE YOU SELLING IT?

Every morning in Africa, a gazelle wakes up. It knows it must run faster than the fastest lion, or it will be killed. Every morning a lion wakes up. It knows it must outrun the slowest gazelle, or it will starve to death. It doesn't matter whether you are a lion or a gazelle. When the sun comes up, you better start running.

—Thomas L. Friedman

The above quotation from Thomas L. Friedman, an American author and three-time Pulitzer Prize winner, has been used countless times in sales meetings and training events, primarily as a way to motivate sales representatives.

However, although the analogy paints a crystal-clear picture of what happens each day, it also exemplifies how sales representatives have been portrayed—and have often portrayed themselves—for more than one hundred years: as active, successful, hungry individuals who will do anything for a sale. They see the prey and they go for the kill!

Unfortunately, this isn't a very beneficial reputation to have, particularly if you make your living in a profession where an unsuccessful "hunt" means that you and your family may not eat.

Andre Roos

The Days of the Snake Oil Salesman

Most of us are familiar with the term "snake oil salesman". Hearing this phrase conjures up images of a seedy profiteer who is trying to exploit an unsuspecting customer with his wares. In the case of historical snake oil salesmen, it was selling fake cures for illnesses.

According to Wikipedia:

> Snake oil, originally a fraudulent liniment without snake extract, has come to refer to any product with questionable or unverifiable quality or benefit. By extension, a snake oil salesman was (or is) someone who knowingly sells fraudulent goods or who is a fraud, quack, or charlatan. The use of snake oil predates the 19th century. In Europe, viper oil had been commonly recommended for many afflictions, including the ones for which rattlesnake oil was subsequently favored. In China, oil made from Chinese water snake fat is a traditional liniment used for treating joint pain. Chinese water snake oil contains 20 percent eicosapentaenoic acid, which has strong analgetic and anti-inflammatory properties.[1]

Due to its supposed healing powers, snake oil was quite popular a century or so ago. Unlike today, it was quite difficult, if not impossible, for customers to test the product and ensure that what they were purchasing was actually what the salesman told them it was. With no Internet or vast array of resources like Google to call upon, the poor prospect had no other option than to believe the salesman as to what the "miracle" snake oil could do. Customers typically didn't realize they had been duped until the snake oil salesman was long gone, and by then it was much too late to obtain a refund.

Much like the reviews we see on the Internet today regarding products, services, and salespeople that buyers should steer clear of, our ancestors tried to call out fraudsters as best they could. One example is this gem of a letter, written in 1905 by Mark Twain to a fraudulent medicine salesman:

Nov. 20, 1905

J. H. Todd

1212 Webster Street

San Francisco, California

Dear Sir,

Your letter is an insoluble puzzle to me. The handwriting is good and exhibits considerable character, and there are even traces of intelligence in what you say, yet the letter and the accompanying advertisements profess to be the work of the same hand. The person who wrote the advertisements is without doubt the most ignorant person now alive on the planet; also without doubt he is an idiot, an idiot of the 33rd degree, and scion of an ancestral procession of idiots stretching back to the Missing Link. It puzzles me to make out how the same hand could have constructed your letter and your advertisements. Puzzles fret me, puzzles annoy me, puzzles exasperate me; and always, for a moment, they arouse in me an unkind state of mind toward the person who has puzzled me. A few moments from now my resentment will have faded and passed and I shall probably even be praying for you; but while there is yet time I hasten to wish that you may take a dose of your own poison by mistake, and enter swiftly into the damnation which you and all other tent medicine assassins have so remorsefully earned and do so richly deserve.

Adieu, adieu, adieu!

Mark Twain [2]

Nowadays, of course, letters like the above have been replaced by 280-character tweets, social media ranting, and other forms of online customer reviews, all of which are equally devastating.

The Changing Landscape of the Sales Profession

While the days of actual snake oil salesmen are thankfully long gone, the perception they created remains today. This is particularly the case in industries where consumers are unfamiliar with the inner workings of the product or service, and they feel like they are being "sold" rather than making a purchase of their own accord. In some cases, consumers even feel pressured to make the purchase, regardless of whether they really need it.

Many old-school sales tactics still in use today are to blame for this feeling of pressure. Using such methods to make a sale can be just as uncomfortable for the sales rep as it is for the consumer. That's not really an ideal way to make a living, is it? Yet the majority of sales trainers today teach these tactics, though for the most part they do not work anymore.

These old-school sales techniques include the following:

- *Pitching your product or service.* You've likely heard the saying, "People who buy a drill don't want a drill; they want a hole." Or "We don't sell the steak, we sell the sizzle." Prospects don't care all that much about your actual product or service, in most cases. Rather, they care very much about the problem it can solve or the benefit it can produce for them. Pitching a product will typically fall on deaf ears and turn the prospect off—even if your offering could indeed help them.

- *Selling to anybody who has a pulse.* Not all products or services are ideal for everyone, even if the sales rep believes that they are. Successful sales representatives don't sell things to everyone they meet. Instead, they offer solutions to people who can truly benefit.

- *Smooth talking to prospects.* Many sales representatives try to sound particularly smooth and polished when they are talking with potential customers. Doing so, they believe, can have the effect of luring a customer in. But consumers don't want to work with a smooth talker any more. Consumers would much prefer to deal with someone who appears real and who educates them about how they can solve a problem or attain a benefit. Given this, it is important to chat with a potential prospect in the same manner that you would with a friend or a co-worker.

- *Being overly enthusiastic about your product or service.* While it is nice to be excited about what you offer, being too keyed up can make you look fake and untrustworthy, leading potential clients to back away. "It sounds too good to be true" is a warning that will sound in a prospect's mind if the salesperson acts overly excited. When something appears too good to be true, it usually is! This can send potential clients running for the exit.

- *Using heavy persuasion.* Heavy persuasion is often the focus of what is taught in sales training. One of the biggest problems with using this sales technique is that you may not be talking with someone who is a good fit for your offering. Persuading them to buy will do them a greater disservice than if you had never spoken with them at all. This will significantly tarnish your reputation as an advisor.

- *Begging a potential client to listen to your proposal.* Yes, this has been an actual sales technique. Sending an unsolicited proposal, or offering it to someone, shows that you assume you already know their needs. But unless you have spent time talking with a prospect, you don't know how or even if your offering will be beneficial to them. Simply offering a proposal out of the blue will likely be a waste of their time as well as yours. Even if the prospect does buy, it is likely they will soon be asking for a refund.

- *Being unclear or secretive regarding the next step.* Often, sales representatives are taught to set an appointment with a prospect by saying something like this: "I'll contact you by phone next Tuesday at 2 p.m. to follow up." The problem with this is that there is no telling whether the prospect will be available, or if they are, what is expected of them. It is almost as if the salesman wants to keep the prospect in the dark, hoping to somehow leverage the element of surprise. This can be a real turn-off to many people.

- *Scaring a prospect into purchasing.* One of the worst sales techniques is using fear. A sales rep may similarly use uncertainty or doubt to get a prospect to buy. Sometimes this is done in order to dissuade an individual from purchasing competing products or services. For example, a salesperson may state that a competitor's insurance company is not financially stable, and because of that, claims may not be paid out to their policyholders. Fear may also be used when discussing one's own product—describing how dreadful the prospect's situation will be unless the salesperson's product or service is purchased. Fear is a popular sales technique among financial advisors. We often hear things like "Find the fear, the hot button. Amplify it, make it real, and then pitch your solution." This is not a good way to go into a relationship with a client—nor is it likely that such a relationship will last very long.

Years ago, when I started my career as an aviation specialist financial advisor, I thought it would be a great idea to use a recent plane crash as a "hot button" to convince a hesitating prospect to sign a policy. Needless to say, the gentleman went from hesitating to being completely annoyed with me within a couple of seconds. I have learned that pilots generally do not like to be reminded about the ever-present risks of their occupation. It took me six months to win back the trust of that prospect. I was lucky that he even considered our relationship again. In many cases, a prospect will run in the other direction and not come back. Never again have I used fear as a sales tactic.

- *Setting a time limit in which to make a decision.* Another popular old-school sales tactic is telling a prospect that they must make a decision before a certain date or time. This may be because the price of your product or service will soon be going up, or because the product may not be available in the future. A looming close-off date for calculating one's commissions often plays a role here as well. This sudden and—from the prospect's perspective, at least—unexplained sense of urgency almost always leaves the prospect with an uneasy feeling. And uneasy prospects usually won't buy.

Yesterday's Sales Tactics Won't Work Today

Throughout the years, sales has changed a great deal. There are many reasons for this, including the following:

- The movement from a product-based economy to a service-based economy
- The movement from local business-to-business sales to a national, even global economy
- The movement from a paper-based environment to an electronic and online environment

- The movement from tightly controlled information to freely available information (in many cases, simply with the touch of a button or the click of a mouse)
- The movement from transactional interactions to relational professional relationships, particularly in the space of insurance and financial services

As these changes in the economy take place, there must also be changes in the way that sales representatives and financial advisors interact with their clients and prospects. Unfortunately, though, we often see these professionals keeping on with "the way it has always been".

Consumers today can see right through a salesperson who is merely trying to make a sale or is offering something that isn't truly beneficial to them, solely to collect the commission (I call them commission wolves). It has become easier to spot snake oil salesmen.

Years ago, I neglected to return a client's email—three emails in a row, in fact—and she wrote her complaint about me on a popular local consumer website. I was at fault, no doubt about it. The very next day, I visited the client with a big bunch of flowers, a humble and apologetic attitude, and a fine bottle of wine. I sorted out the problem, and I am happy to report that to this day, the client is still my client. Unfortunately, she neglected to remove her complaint for at least thirteen months. The complaint appeared on the first page of all major search engines if a prospect searched my name. Who knows how much damage that one complaint caused me?

Is Technology Rendering Your Sales Job Redundant (and Therefore Unnecessary)?

In many ways, then, the job of a pure salesman may actually be disappearing; hence the title of this book. Thanks in large part to today's technology, sales representatives can follow up with leads who have already shown some interest in a product or service. This is because the consumer has either asked for more information, or the consumer has downloaded information about the offering online.

Today, there are also sales funnels online that will take an individual from an expression of interest in a product to a closed sale simply by typing some key words into a search engine. Because of the ease and convenience of this type of process, many consumers are purchasing products in this manner. Unfortunately, many end up sacrificing quality and the right fit for the sake of saving a bit of time.

As an example, a few weeks ago I made what is considered a major purchase. No, not a property, but a motor vehicle. The entire deal took less than seven minutes. The only role that the salesman played was in filling out the paperwork and helping to source the colour I wanted.

What the salesman didn't know was that it took me three months to decide on the right vehicle for my complex family needs. I considered every seven-seater SUV on the market, I watched YouTube videos about them, and I studied all of the reviews. I compared price and value, along with guarantees and financing options. I even studied future demand and resale value for the vehicle. The salesman played no role in my education at all. The receptionist could have closed the deal.

In our modern world, though technology can be highly beneficial in getting information across, it cannot completely replace the skill involved in becoming a trusted advisor to the client. I believe this is because financial advice is not a sales but a service industry, and the rules for the two are completely different. When it comes to service, it is essential to establish a valued and trusted relationship with the prospects and clients you serve.

Financial Advice—The Ultimate Relationship Business

Although there are sales representatives in virtually every industry, nowhere is building relationships more important than with financial advice. According to the Oxford English Dictionary, a relationship is defined as "the way in which two or more concepts, objects, or people are connected, or the state of being connected," and also as "the way in which two or more people or organizations regard and behave toward each other."

In order to remain competitive in a now borderless world, it is imperative for insurance professionals to step away from old-school sales techniques and foster trusted, valued relationships with those they serve.

Having or not having the proper insurance, as most of us are well aware, can make the difference between financially covering an unexpected event and bearing the responsibility yourself. Even if a client does some research online, they could still end up purchasing the wrong coverage for their particular needs. This would not likely happen if they were working directly with a trusted advisor who was well versed in the field and knew the long list of extenuating circumstances that could occur.

Customers have a wide array of options to choose from, starting with the agent or broker they work with. Why should a client choose you over the many other alternatives? One of the biggest differentiators is how you communicate with them. How do you listen to and help solve their needs? Are you perceived as an invaluable resource?

Strive to Be in "the One Third"

In a world that is filled with diversity, there is a plethora of ideas, values, and thought processes. According to the "one third, two thirds" principle, we are statistically likely to get along with roughly one third of the people we meet—those whom we consider to be most like us. The other two thirds, not so much. It is possible to be transactional with the two thirds, but the general consensus is that it is not possible to be sincerely relational.

Back in the days of the snake oil salesman, this principle didn't really apply. Those sales representatives sold their offering to anyone who was willing to listen. After making the sale, the sales rep moved on without any intention of coming back. There was no need to build up a relationship with the client, or even to like the client at all.

When considering the one third, two thirds principle today, it is important to keep in mind that, even though you don't get along ideally with two thirds of those you meet, you can work the remaining third and become a trusted advisor to them. You don't need to spend time trying to convert the other two-thirds.

How will you know who falls into the one third and who falls into the two thirds? One of the best ways to determine this is to interview a prospect to ascertain whether they are compatible with you. That may determine whether the foundation for a long and trusted advisor relationship can exist.

If so, great! It is here that you will want to spend the bulk of your time and effort, growing, enhancing, and maintaining the relationship over the long term.

If the person you interview falls into the two-thirds component, then you can still keep a cordial acquaintance and introduce them to another advisor who has a better chance of falling into their one-third category.

While this relationship building may be a different approach from what most clients are used to, it is typically very well received. It is a process that clients will grow to anticipate in all of their business endeavours going forward.

So how can you convert from working with whoever comes along to building a more valued relationship?

Read on!

***

Success Action Steps

Trust-oriented advisors are able to build client relationships quickly and successfully by removing tasks and mannerisms that imply a sales mentality, and replacing them with actions that demonstrate value.

With that in mind, take some time and conduct an audit of your practice. Remove everything that looks like sales, including jargon in your marketing materials and in your speech. Consider some rebranding of your old terminology. For example, a sales manager might now be referred to as a business coach. A sales meeting can be called an activity meeting. Clients may become relationships.

Additional Action Steps

By building a practice on valued relationships, you will be better able to attract the potential clients you want to work with and keep the clients you currently have. It is possible, though, that before you transition to relationship-based advising, you will have some clients who are in the two-thirds component that will never move beyond a transactional connection with you.

Take some time to go through your entire client list. Decipher which individuals are among your ideal third and which fall into the two thirds who may be better served by another agent.

Although it can be difficult to give up certain clients—and the income that is associated with them—in the long run, doing so will free up more of your time to focus on building trusted relationships with those that are ideal for you and you for them.

CHAPTER 2

THE ROSETO EFFECT

We see our customers as invited guests to a party, and we are the hosts. It's our job every day to make every important aspect of the customer experience a little bit better.

—Jeff Bezos, CEO of Amazon.com

Today, due in large part to the vast reach of the Internet, consumers have a myriad of options when it comes to purchasing most any product or service that they want. Gone are the days when an insurance advisor sat across the kitchen table from his clients and determined a family's specific need for coverage. Direct insurance providers and telesales companies are particularly notorious for "removing the middleman" to add more value, or so they say.

Rather, items and services are often purchased without any customer contact at all. In the short term, this may provide ease and convenience to the buyer. But in the longer term, it can—and I believe that it will—leave both the customer and the provider completely segregated from one another.

The Importance of Social Networks

Over the past decade or so, you would be hard pressed to find anyone who is not at least somewhat familiar with social networks. Facebook, Twitter, Instagram, and Pinterest all hold a great deal of significance for millions of people. Many spend an inordinate amount of time on one or even all of these on-line platforms. But do these networks truly embrace the meaning of the word "social"?

While many would answer that question with a resounding yes, the reality is that in a number of different ways, online social networks have actually taken people further away from relating to each other in meaningful, healthy ways. One of the best demonstrations of this is the Roseto effect.

The Roseto Effect

For thousands of years, people have been nourished by other people through live, personal relationships, not the ones we create and maintain only via a smartphone screen. The importance of live social networks and interaction, in terms of health, happiness, and longevity, has been confirmed by a study of a close-knit Italian-American community, from which researchers have derived what is known as the Roseto effect. At one time, the village of Roseto, Pennsylvania, was a living laboratory demonstrating that neighbourliness is good, not just for the body politic (i.e., the community), but for the human body as well.

What exactly is the Roseto effect? It is defined as "the phenomenon by which a close-knit community experiences a reduced rate of heart disease." In the mid-1900s, two medical professionals discovered an unusually low rate of myocardial infarction in Roseto as compared to other locations around the country. It was surmised that the middle-aged male residents of Roseto had lower rates of adverse heart conditions due, in large part, to their lower-than-average stress levels, even though many of these men "smoked unfiltered stogies, drank wine 'with seeming abandon',[1] did not typically follow a healthy eating plan, and many worked in slate quarries, which regularly subjected them to dust and harmful gases."[2] In fact, the citizens of this particular community died of heart attacks at a rate of only half that of the rest of the United States. This was bewildering to medical researchers, as it essentially defied all previous medical logic.

So why did these individuals incur a lower rate of adverse heart conditions?

According to one of the researchers, "The community...was very cohesive. There was no keeping up with the Joneses. Houses were very close together, and everyone lived more or less alike."[3]

In their book *The Roseto Story*, John Bruhn and Steward Wolf give a fascinating account of the research that was done in Roseto and the results of that research. All of the houses contained three generations of family.

While there was no genetic or other physical explanation for this much lower death rate, there was some additional information that was eye-catching to the researchers: both that the crime rate and the applications for public assistance in Roseto were zero.

Subsequent study showed that all of the houses in Roseto contained three generations of family, providing real-life proof that Rosetans took care of their own. Rather than putting their elderly residents "on the shelf", the town elevated, respected, cared for, and revered its seniors.

The study led researchers to conclude that the Roseto effect of healthier hearts had much less to do with something seen via a microscope, and much more to do with the town's sense of community. The family dinner tables, the evening strolls, the many social clubs, and the church festivals contributed measurably to the residents' good health.

In a later study titled "The Power of the Clan", conducted by the same medical researchers, it was concluded that mutual respect and cooperation can and do contribute to the health and welfare of a community and its inhabitants. Further, self-indulgence and lack of concern for others can exert the exact opposite influences.

Other studies from England have shown that the highest rate of death from coronary heart disease occurs among civil servants who have the least social support. So we are indeed nourished by having contact with others.

The people in Roseto formed a close-knit community. Possibly the strongest conformity in the village was the work ethic. Not only did residents work together, but they also worked towards a common goal, which was to provide a better life for their children. In the slate quarries and blouse factories, the men and women of Roseto laboured to send their children to college—which they did at a rate that exceeded the national average, even though they were not affluent by American standards.

A healthier heart isn't the only benefit of close-knit community and good, solid relationships. There is also striking evidence of a correlation between mental health, and even a person's overall well-being. For example, the highest rates of tuberculosis have been found among isolated and marginal people who have little social support, even though these individuals may live in affluent neighbourhoods.

The overall atmosphere of Roseto was one of close and mutually supportive family relationships. This cohesive quality extended to neighbours and the community as a whole.[5] For example, each night of the week, almost everyone in town ate the same food for dinner. This conformity tended to reduce the feeling of distance between the "haves" and the "have nots".[4]

According to anthropologist David Maybury-Lewis, individuals in a tribal society grow up in a defined world, where people know their place and their relationship to others. Conversely, when an individual grows up with freedom and in a limitless world, they are often lost and terribly alone.

Why does this have meaning for an advisor's practice?

The benefits of social bonds actually have a great deal to do with becoming a trusted advisor,[5] including the strength and quality of the clients you attract to and keep in your book of business. And in turn, this relates to how long you are likely to retain certain clients in your book, and even to the total number of clients you should or should not have.

Transactional versus Relational—And Why It Matters

At first blush, Roseto seems to show a diorama of what once was the nation's ideal lifestyle. Neighbours looked after one another, and civic-minded joiners and doers formed the grass roots of American democracy.

Those virtues have all but disappeared. Due in large part to our infatuation with technology, we have become a nation of strangers. When you take a look around you, it is likely that you'll see people interacting with a smartphone or a tablet, not speaking a word to each other.

The Death of the Salesman and the Rise of the Trusted Financial Advisor

Roseto was not immune to the technological revolution. Life changed there too. The above-referenced study took place just as Roseto's golden age of community was drawing to a close. The researchers were able to predict, even back in the 1960s, that Rosetans under the age of 30 would not long be content with their rigid, traditional lifestyle.

By the 1970s, homes on the outskirts of Roseto were being built in the suburbanized style that had become the American norm: large, single-family houses with fenced yards and swimming pools. Churches became located outside of the community. As people moved and achieved more material success, they found that success at the expense of the traditional, communal values with which they had been raised. One resident said, "I'm sorry we moved. Everything is modern here and we have everything I need here ... except people."[6]

Even the elementary school principal noted that the lives of the children of Roseto had drastically changed. In earlier times, the children had spent their time doing activities and socializing with each other. Today, the children tended to "watch life from the sidelines".[7] The principal had to teach the modern children how to play marbles and jacks.

The strongest evidence that change had come in the town of Roseto was when the town's coronet band, which was founded in 1890, demanded for the first time to be paid for playing at the church's big festival.

As medical researchers continued to monitor the village, they noted that, while Americans' vulnerability to heart attack began to decline overall, the rate of heart issues in Roseto began to rise.

Again, why does the story of the Roseto effect have any bearing at all on your advisory practice? The Roseto effect clearly demonstrates that as humans, we are designed to live in communities and not alone. In many ways, we are pack animals, and therefore we rely on and trust each other as part of our overall well-being.

It is possible that you have a number of current clients with whom you have only a professional relationship. You work to take care of their insurance or financial needs. There is nothing negative about this, per se. However, it is possible that the client purchased from you based on product or price alone. This can make for a shaky advisor-client relationship, particularly if a better product or a lower price becomes available somewhere else, as it inevitably will.

A transactional relationship with a client can often be compared to simply filling an order. The relationship is often not built upon a strong foundation, and because of that, it can quickly and easily fall apart. A transactional relationship is always open to a better deal. Your offering is a commodity to the client, and it can be replaced.

Advisors who have truly relational associations with their clients know who their clients are and what is important to them, including their families, their jobs, their dreams, and their goals, in addition to their intricate needs. A relational advisor also knows how to adapt for the changes that will inevitably take place in clients' lives down the road. In fact, the advisor can sometimes anticipate those changes before they occur. This is the sign of a truly trusted advisor, and a relationship that will be indispensable to the client throughout the years.

Transitioning from a Transactional to a Relational Practice

Even with all of the social media outlets at our disposal today, many people experience loneliness. An isolated person can often become overwhelmed, even by the issues of everyday life. When such a person internalizes that feeling as stress, it can in turn adversely affect just about everything, from blood pressure to kidney function. Such adverse effects are less likely to be the outcome when a person is surrounded by caring friends, neighbours, and relatives, as well as by trusted advisors.

Trusted advisors understand that the best way to help their clients is by owning the voice of those clients and being relational in nature. One way to ensure that you become a trusted advisor to those with whom you are best suited to work is to pare down your overall book of business and work with the third of prospects with whom you fit well, allowing another advisor to take on the other two thirds.

While this complex and unusual approach may initially seem counterproductive, in reality it can produce the best results for all involved. Remember that the two thirds is the people whom you don't like and don't get along with anyway. It is almost impossible to build a trust relationship with such a client. Therefore, it is in your interest and the interest of the client for the client to rather find an advisor they like and are more likely to build a relationship with.

No matter how good you are at your job, there will always be people who don't like you. It is no big deal. Get over it! Don't keep a client simply for the sake of your ego.

Can You Have Too Many Clients?

When building up an insurance or financial advisory practice, advisors often assume that anyone and everyone is a potential client. This is not the case at all. Advisors are well aware that having no clients at all equates to having no income, but is there such a thing as having too many clients in your book?

In a word, yes.

According to Dunbar's number, there is a maximum limit to the number of social relationships that a human being can maintain. This number is estimated to be between 120 to 150 people, on average. It corresponds not only to the number of people that modern people have one-on-one relationships with, but also to the average size of ancient villages and the size of Roman regiments.[6]

Simply stated, when humans needed to stick together for survival many years ago, it was typically possible to handle a maximum group size of about one hundred and fifty. Beyond that, human brains could not keep track of everyone.[7] The same concept still holds true today.

Therefore, while many advisors, especially those who have been in business for many years, may have a thousand or more clients on their books, the reality is as few as one hundred and twenty trusted professional client relationships can be difficult to maintain. A list of a thousand is no longer comprised of clients; they are often just names.

For a client to really be a client, the advisor should know all the needs of the person, from the person's will right through to their grandkids' education planning—anything and everything that falls within the advisor's mandate. Some believe that even as few as thirty-five clients would be a challenging list to build this kind of deep and long-lasting relationships with.

So what does this tell us about maintaining a practice that provides service from a trusted advisor who truly knows each client? First, it tells us that in order to be efficient and offer clients the best advice possible, it is difficult, if not impossible, to maintain much more than one hundred and twenty relationships in your book.

It also tells us that an advisor should never rely on the quality of one's offering alone to retain the relationship with a client, even if that product or service is highly unique. Products go through cycles, as do prices, and it is only a matter of time before something better or cheaper comes along. That's when you are likely to lose your transactional clients. At that point, you find yourself constantly having to defend your book instead of building your practice.

But what if you purposely trimmed down your client base to a hundred and twenty or fewer, so that you could devote quality time to those with whom you have built relationships? What if you referred your transactional clients to newer advisors who are in need of income and agree to a commission-sharing arrangement? In many ways, this could be a win-win-win situation for all.

Think about it this way: if you have clients that you really are not providing service for, you are doing the client, your company, and yourself a disservice by keeping those clients in your book. By shifting them over to a new advisor, you give advisor and client an opportunity to build a relationship, and you can focus on the clients in your book who fit your practice best.

Needless to say, the new advisor would love the opportunity to add some clients to their growing book, and would no doubt look after the client far better than you would have been able to do. If this pass-on is done professionally, in most cases the client will have no problem with it. Hopefully, the client will end up with an advisor who falls in the third of people the client can build a relationship with.

When this realization hit me, I decided to pass about 420 of my clients on to new advisors. I must be honest—the decision took me a good six months to finally make, and a further three months to execute. Why? Because of the fear of losing income, and also because of a weird emotional connection I felt towards each client. My thought was, "I worked hard for them, so I am keeping them no matter what."

Once I made the decision, I emailed and called the clients to explain what I was doing and why I was doing it. I then introduced them to the new advisors I recommended. Much to my surprise, not one of the clients complained. Most of them praised me for what they called a bold move, one they clearly perceived as putting their needs in front of my own.

The result has been that I now write more business with my eighty remaining clients than I did with over five hundred. As an added bonus, I seem to have a lot less stress. I also find myself being far more intentional, thorough, and strategic with my remaining clients. This too is a win for all.

Information Overload?

The number factor can also come into play when given a plethora of options for our clients to choose from. Studies have shown that the more options you give to a person, the less likely they are to make a decision. This is called the "paradox of choice".[8] For instance, if given twenty options to choose from, an individual is highly likely not to choose any. If you provide the same individual with only three potential solutions, they are roughly 95 per cent likely to make a decision.[9]

Now imagine that you are standing on one side of a river, and you want to safely get to the other side. There are five bridges you can choose from. You are unsure which will actually get you there safely. There are a number of people on the other side of the river, and each of them is shouting an opinion about which bridge is safest. If you notice a long-time friend in the crowd, and that friend is telling you to take bridge 3, it is almost guaranteed that this is the bridge you will take.

A similar effect can be seen when advisory clients are given too many choices. Even a major decision such as obtaining risk insurance can be put off if a client has too many options. So how can you provide your clients with the information that they need, without giving them too much?

The best way, I believe, is to become a trusted advisor who truly knows the client. Aim to become someone who is considered by the client as a member of their community. Then, when information overload is present, the client will revert to the habits built into human genetic design—habits that value community.

Becoming a Truly Relational Advisor

By our very nature, humans are meant to survive and thrive by having a true sense of community. This is the case in our personal relationships as well as for our business relationships. Taking the necessary steps towards working only with those you were meant to serve can seem a bit harsh, at least initially. But in the long run, it can turn out to be a winning situation for all involved.

***

Success Action Steps

Building a relational practice can help ensure that clients value your advice far beyond the products or services that you offer. A relational practice can also cement the relationship clients have with you, and you with them.

To move from a transactional to a relational practice, first read through your list of clients and rate each one in terms of how relational you are with them. Be sure to take into account whether you really know the client and are familiar with the following factors. Answer each with a yes or no.

You know the client's:
- _____ Spouse
- _____ Children
- _____ Parents
- _____ Closest Friends
- _____ Goals (short- and long-term)
- _____ Hobbies
- _____ Favourite sports and teams
- _____ Other advisors
- _____ Attorney
- _____ Accountant
- _____ Doctor or medical advisor(s)
- _____ Spiritual advisor

The Death of the Salesman and the Rise of the Trusted Financial Advisor

The following additional factors should also be considered:

_____ You have been invited to the client's home.

_____ You have been invited to the client's place of business.

_____ You have been invited to special events in the client's life (such as holiday celebrations, weddings, funerals).

_____ You have been invited to sporting events by the client, either as spectator or participant.

_____ You have been asked to give advice on something outside of your mandate, as for example a property purchase.

Once you have completed this checklist for each of your clients, the next step is to rank them according to which ones you truly have a relational bond with, and which are more transactional and may be better served by another advisor.

CHAPTER 3

EFFECTIVE SALES SUICIDE TECHNIQUES

The truth in our world is very rare, and, because of that, it has the tactical element of surprise. It's been my experience that the surprise, much more often than not, leads to very positive results. In selling, in relationships, and in life.

—Anonymous

From the moment we are born, we are all involved, one way or another, in sales. As a child, you likely tried to sell your parents on reasons why you wanted (or "needed") a new toy. According to the US Bureau of Labor Statistics, one in nine Americans works in sales.[1] This means that every day, roughly fifteen million people in the US earn their living by persuading someone else to make a purchase.

But according to Daniel Pink, author of the book *To Sell is Human*, while one in nine Americans may be acknowledged as working in sales, so do the other eight! In fact, most of us spend our days trying to move others. Often, this involves the client parting with a certain sum in return for the product or service that you are offering.

Whether or not we accomplish our goal will depend largely upon our approach, which can have a great deal to do with how we are ultimately perceived by prospects, clients, and anyone else we interact with. For those who work in a competitive field like insurance or financial services, there have long been sales techniques in place that are designed to move prospects closer to a sale.

Depending on how long you have been in the field, it is possible that you have been taught obsolete yet still commonly used sales techniques.

Some sales trainers taught salespeople how to study a prospect's body language. Other approaches, like neuro-linguistic programming (NLP), claim there is a connection between neurological processes, language, and behavioural patterns that are learned through experience and can be changed in order to achieve specific goals.

Many of these methods did their job in years gone by. Some are nothing other than ways to manipulate clients into buying, regardless of whether they will benefit from your offering or not.

In my opinion, such tricks are not the way to build a trusted relationship with clients. Even if an individual buys from you once, they will end up jumping ship as soon as they feel that their needs are more appropriately met elsewhere.

The Rise of the Well-Informed Prospect

Outdated and manipulative sales techniques are often uncomfortable for salespeople to perform. Such methods are also easily spotted by a prospect, which can make an advisor seem pushy and untrustworthy. Nowadays, clients and prospects are so well-informed that these manipulative techniques are considered *sales suicide*. In other words, by using them, the advisor is killing the sale (not to mention one's reputation) rather than moving it forward.

Usually when a prospect picks up on this approach, they refuse to proceed to a meeting and, of course, the sale. Even if the prospect only picks it up on a subconscious level, they will still feel uncomfortable. Depending on the individual, they may even speak out against the advisor, using word of mouth or one of the far-reaching social media platforms that are available today. Why? Well, nobody wants to be manipulated or lied to.

Consider for a moment that you are seeking a financial advisor to work with. As you read through information that is easily available via the Internet, you will likely see that some advisors have received highly positive testimonials from clients, while other advisors are reviewed in terms that are not so nice. Which advisors are you more willing to gravitate towards?

On top of that, in the regulation-heavy world of insurance and financial services, advisors can face stiff penalties for infractions, ranging from monetary fines to loss of their license to practice to jail time for the most egregious offenses.

Given these risks, what is the point of manipulating a prospect into buying an intangible product that can be cancelled at any time, at a cost to you of a chargeback of your commission? It should go without saying that doing what is best for your client is the best course of action to take all around, for them and for you.

Caveat Emptor Is No More

Caveat emptor is a Latin phrase that means "let the buyer beware". It is a warning that buyers should assume that they are taking all of the risk in a transaction. The phrase initially had to do with the sale of real estate, and has come to be well known across a variety of other industries, including insurance and financial services.

Under the legal principle of caveat emptor, a purchaser was not able to recover any damages from the seller for defects that rendered a purchase unfit for ordinary purposes.[1] Though laws have changed over time with regard to the products and services affected by caveat emptor, many buyers still feel compelled to be cautious, especially in higher-ticket transactions.

Skip the Sales Script and Increase Success

Imagine answering the telephone and hearing the following words: "Hello <Name>. How are you?"

You respond with the obligatory, "Fine."

The caller proceeds to delve into the features of whatever it is he is selling, regardless of whether it is a good fit for your needs.

Although you may be polite when you tell the caller, "No, thank you," it could be that you get so irritated by this intrusion, you slam the phone down while the caller is still in mid-sentence. Either way, it is highly unlikely that you will run to grab your money and immediately purchase whatever it is that this person is hoping to sell you.

Sales "tracks", or scripts, are used in any number of industries, from pre-owned vehicles to electronics to insurance products. Most scripts used in the insurance field in the past had various avenues for the salesperson to follow, depending on which way the prospect took the conversation. For example, if the prospect presented an objection to the affordability of a policy, the script's solution was to state that there was a policy available for just about any budget—making no mention of whether the coverage was right for the prospect's needs: "The good news is that we can find you a policy for practically any budget. So let's get you started. What is your full name and address?"

Or perhaps the prospect protested that that he was crunched for time. The salesperson would press onward with a response like this: "No problem. We can complete your application very quickly. And by doing it now, you will actually save time in the long run. Now, how would you like your name to appear on the policy?"

In order to close more sales, salespeople were typically taught to give the prospect a choice between two or three options. Rather than giving the prospect an opportunity to flat-out say no, the salesperson guided the prospect towards one of the alternatives: "If you had to pick one, which of the three policies I've presented do you think would fit your needs best?" Once the prospect, often reluctantly, stated a preference, the sales representative would continue: "Great. That would be my pick as well. Now, I just need to get some basic information. What is the proper spelling of your name?"

I am sure as you were reading this, you recalled having conversations like this and the feelings associated with them, regardless of which end of the phone you were on. Today, prospects will quickly hang up the phone if they hear anything even remotely similar to this. They know quite well that the salesperson is just trying to sell them something, regardless of their true needs. Moving away from a sales script is absolutely necessary if you want to become a trusted advisor.

Advisory Board

I have always been of the opinion that we ought to be comfortable having our top clients sit right next to us in *all* of our sales meetings. In fact, I sometimes imagine that I have a few clients in the room. Then afterwards I ask myself these questions: How did the clients perceive the meeting? Would they now be more inclined or less inclined to do business with my firm? What would they tell their friends and family after their "insider experience" with me?

What if you set up an advisory board that was entirely made up of your firm's clients? I am sure that this has never happened, but just imagine the many benefits it could have. After all, is our business not all about our clients? Without them, we would not have a business, so why not let them have a say in our firms?

We spend fortunes in sales gatherings and company meetings, trying to ascertain what clients want and how our target markets will respond. But why not just ask them directly? Wouldn't that make things much easier and more beneficial for everyone involved?

Don't be afraid to expose the inner workings of your company to your clients. Doing so could turn out to be the best thing that happens to them and you.

Force No Sale

Like all entrepreneurs, advisors need to earn a living. From time to time, finances might be tight. Personal financial pressure puts additional pressure on the advisor to do the right thing and not put one's own interest before the interest of the client. To pressure a client to make a decision will almost always end in a negative reply, not to mention potential reputational damage.

Your financial situation is of no concern to your client. Therefore, if your commission close-off is two days away, it is certainly not the client's problem. The client should never be pressured to make a decision because you need your commission. I have come across advisors who actually tell their clients that they need to process the paperwork before a certain day so that they can get paid. This, I believe, is unacceptable. It creates a bad impression of the advisor, the advisor's company, and the industry as a whole.

A trusted advisor can never be that desperate for a commission. Trust me when I say that I know what it feels like to sit in front of a client, aware that if the client doesn't sign right now, there will be no money to pay the rent. I know it, and it is very real. However, I will never, ever show it to the client in any form whatsoever. What the client sees is a cool, calm, confident, and successful financial advisor who is appreciative of but certainly not desperate for business.

Years ago, when I was working in sales for another industry, I used my last bit of money for fuel to drive to a meeting with a client, knowing that I wouldn't have enough fuel to make it back home. I had to make the deal and get the client to pay cash for his purchase. To make matters worse, the client had a thirty-day statement account with my company.

Regardless, I still sat in front of the client with a confident and professional attitude. I was someone who was by no means desperate for anybody's business. In fact, I acted somewhat reluctant even to place my goods in the client's store. The power of negotiation was on my side of the table—even though I had absolutely no money in my bank account. It was not easy, that I promise you.

We made the deal. On my way out, I stopped in the doorway and mentioned that I had a 5 percent cash settlement discount policy, and that another client, his opposition, a few blocks away, had not taken those terms. Needless to say, the client paid me in cash right then and there, and I had money to go home and carry on with my business.

I have no doubt that if I had disclosed my dire situation to the client, he would not have bought my products. Successful people want to deal with other successful people. Success breeds success.

I believe it is very important to conduct yourself in a confident and professional manner, no matter what is in your bank account. Our bank accounts should make no difference to how trusted advisors conduct themselves.

Moving Forward with Purpose

Over the past decade or so, the sales profession has moved away from a world of caveat emptor to one that is more *caveat venditor*, or "seller beware". Honesty, fairness, and transparency are often the only viable path.[2] Discarding questionable and outdated sales techniques will help you turn into a true professional who is seen by clients and prospects as a trusted advisor—not someone who is simply out for a pay cheque!

Though all trusted professionals must start somewhere, going about it by using an impersonal sales technique like telephone scripts will only prove frustrating for you and those whom you approach. A much better way is to start from wherever you are right now and implement skills that will prove you don't always have to be closing sales, but rather getting to know people's true needs and then solving them.

Have you ever thought about the odds of making a successful phone call, especially a cold call? What is the chance of somebody selling *you* something over the phone? To make a successful call, a number of things must be in perfect alignment:

1. The prospect must be in a good frame of mind—not stressed out, not depressed, not angry, not worried, and not having just realized that their spouse is cheating.
2. The prospect must have time to talk to you. Remember that a phone call is always an interruption in someone's day. How often do we have time to attentively listen to a complete stranger over the phone? If the answer for you is "almost never", then you understand that the answer of your prospect would be the same, assuming that you are not canvassing from an unemployed list.
3. The prospect must have recently thought about purchasing your specific product or service.

There are more factors that should ideally be present too, but the odds of just these three being in line and favourable must be off the charts.

Now you must also consider human behaviour. Who would do the same thing over and over if there were no or very few results? A small minority of people have that kind of resilience. Most salespeople look for a better alternative that gives immediate results. Results are a very strong motivator. Results breed motivation and, in turn, more and more results. Sadly, though, many very skilled insurance and financial advisors are forced to make hundreds of cold calls each workday. In the absence of a better alternative, they leave the industry.

Now that we have gone over how *not* to approach your potential customers, we will take a close look at how to move away from scripted sales pitches. Let's kill the sales suicide techniques once and for all, and work towards becoming experts whom people seek out.

***

Success Action Steps

Stepping away from using a sales script may be difficult, particularly if you have relied upon this technique for some time, or if you are brand-new to the industry. However, by making the break, you will be in a much better position to be perceived as a trusted advisor by clients and prospects.

With that in mind, go through your current sales training materials and remove anything that even remotely resembles a script. This can reduce the temptation to continue using it.

Next, consider how you deal with your clients: If there is anything in your approach that is even remotely manipulative, get rid of it immediately. You should use no manipulation at all in your dealings with prospects and clients. It is really just that simple.

Ask yourself this question: How would you feel if you realized that the person you entrusted the future of your loved ones to was in fact manipulating you?

Trusted advisors are *trusted*.

CHAPTER 4

SALES COURTESY

Courtesy is as much a mark of a gentleman as courage.

—Theodore Roosevelt

When shopping for products and services that you need, you have undoubtedly had both positive and negative experiences. Some of these may have led you to retain the provider for the purchase of future goods and services, or alternatively, to never return to that provider again (and perhaps to advise your family and friends not to use them either).

Customer courtesy refers to a variety of informal behaviours that are demonstrated by a company or its representatives, which can have a key impact on the customer's experience. It is essential to ensure that those whom you wish to retain as clients have only the utmost in positive contact with you.

Trusted Advisor Supply and Demand

If you have taken any economics courses, then you are likely familiar with the concepts of supply and demand. When sought after items are in short supply, and there is a great demand for it then prices will rise, of course if there is an over-supply of the item or the demand drops then

The Death of the Salesman and the Rise of the Trusted Financial Advisor

the price is likely to drop as well. This concept can be used not only with physical, tangible products, but also with services that are perceived as having a high value to clients.

In Cape Town, South Africa, there exists a hamburger restaurant where the burgers are quite good, but nothing really extraordinary. Yet because this establishment only makes sixty hamburgers per day, and the restaurant closes once the sixtieth burger has been sold, there is an acute issue of supply and demand there. So much so that, in order to get your hands on one of their hamburgers, it is necessary to get in queue by 4 p.m., though the doors don't open until five. Otherwise, you will be out of luck.

This restaurant is owned by a rather eccentric English gentleman. I did the math and he is no doubt making a decent living, which he is accomplishing by working only a couple of hours per day. In many ways, the guy is a genius. To be honest, I kind of envy him. What a lifestyle!

So what does this Cape Town restaurant have to do with the successful running of an insurance practice? Actually, quite a bit. When you limit your practice to just one hundred and twenty clients, for example, you will create an issue of supply and demand too. The supply and demand issue will be for your time and advisory services.

When this takes place, it will equate to a win-win situation for you and those who you take on to advise. Imagine how this will change the sales call if you are in fact interviewing the prospect to see *if they qualify* for the few client positions you have left open.

In this situation, it is important to relay to the prospect right up front that you are limited in the number of individuals that you can take on, and therefore you want to ensure that the two of you are a good fit for working together. I have tried and tested this supply and demand concept for many years and have never found a client who complained about it. Even those who were not initially considered a good fit appreciated the honesty.

As you move forward through this process, there is no need to manipulate or try to sell anything. You simply explain to the prospect how your business works and what can be expected from the relationship going forward, including key criteria such as:

- how you get paid

- how commissions are determined
- how the overall process works

You then turn your focus to the client by asking pertinent questions and intently listening to what the prospect says—not so you can formulate a reply, but rather so that you can better determine what the prospect's needs and expectations are. The conversation will also be beneficial in determining where the prospect falls in terms of being in your one third of people who are a good fit.

In some cases, you will be able to help. In others, you may not be able to solve the prospect's issues. Figuring this out up front will save both of you years of a bad fit.

The secret here is not to sell the prospect anything at all. You are gently guiding the prospect towards discovering the solution (or solutions) for themselves. Right from the start, it is essential that you tell the prospect that you are just going to discuss the issues, and that once these are clear, the two of you will move on to collectively coming up with viable solutions. You will be amazed how this puts the prospect at ease.

All the while, you should be focused on making sure that the prospect is comfortable. Getting a prospect agitated may lead to them leaving before getting to a solution.

Years ago, I made a sales call on one of my trusted, long-time clients. He and I had been out together to many social events, and we were at the point that we considered each other friends.

That day, something was obviously wrong. He normally ordered a wide range of my products, and I normally spent at least ninety minutes in his shop. Now I found him extremely eager to get me out of his shop. I was puzzled by his strange behaviour.

Then he took a phone call. While he was occupied, I started looking around his shop for possible clues that could explain the situation. Perhaps he had taken a large special shipment from an opposition company?

I peeked into the shop kitchen and noticed a half-finished plate of food. There on the kitchen counter sat the reason why my client was not ordering any stock—he was hungry! I promptly excused myself from his store with a promise to return later that afternoon. Needless to say, he happily agreed. Later that afternoon, we had a great time and he placed a large order with me.

Had I not noticed that something was bothering him, I stood the risk of not just losing the order, but damaging the relationship with him altogether. The lesson here: be observant! If a client or prospect isn't ready to purchase, don't push them. Their behaviour in the moment may not mean that they don't want your product. They may simply not be ready to talk about it.

It is also important, when vying to be seen as a trusted advisor, that you do away with some "tried and true" sales techniques, such as the following:

- *Closing a sale versus making a collective decision:* For years, anyone in a sales position has been taught to follow certain "rules." One such rule is referred to as ABC, or "always be closing". But the reality is that today, consumers are keen on knowing when they are being sold rather than being listened to by a trusted advisor who truly has their best interests at heart.
- *Observation of body language*: In many traditional sales processes, representatives are instructed to be cognizant of a client's body language and to try to mimic it. Years ago I invented a word for it—I called it "chameleonize", more commonly known as *mirroring*.

  For example, one technique advises that the sales representative, "Start off largely reflecting [the client] back, by matching body language and using similar verbal style, in order to create an emotional bond with them."[1]

  Some sales disciplines advise a salesperson to lean in towards the client. That way, the salesperson will supposedly be creating a deeper bond with the client and getting closer to them.[2] This, however, is not the case at all when you are working to become a trusted advisor.

  While it is important to observe the client in order to determine whether they may be getting uncomfortable, matching body language and leaning in is not the answer. Rather, if it appears that the client is not comfortable, stop the need-related questions and ask if all is OK.

It could be that the client is simply running short on time or has other concerns to contend with at that moment. By being courteous and respecting the client's needs, you can open up the platform for discussion. The client will respect the fact that you are not just trying to force a sale. I cannot stress enough the importance of rapport building. Take your time, respect the client, and work on building a solid foundation for your relationship.

- *Effectively listening to the client's needs*: In most any sales training, it is said that advisors should listen to their clients. But what occurs after that can literally make or break your chance of becoming a trusted advisor.

  Really listen to what the client is saying before you even begin to respond. In doing so, you will be much better able to decipher the client's wants and needs, and to move forward together to find an agreeable solution. Great listening skills are well worth pursuing and mastering; they will change not only your career but your life. While listening to your client, be sure that you pay attention to their:

  - past experiences with the financial services industry
  - past experiences with any previous advisor
  - expectations of you
  - possible concerns
  - understanding of the value that you can deliver
  - primary reason for sitting in front of you

The last point is important. The client will always have a reason for agreeing to an initial meeting. Get to that reason as soon as possible and use it as the cornerstone for the relationship.

Note that the issues I have listed are not comprehensive or conclusive. They are only the starting point of your discovering with the client.

Discovering

Many companies make use of *discovering templates*. These are documents that have been carefully designed to guide the advisor to ask the right questions and gather all of the necessary information in order to compile a proper financial needs analysis. Normally, these templates are three to four pages long and contain multiple questions that could assist the advisor to mine the client for other referrals—for example, a boss, doctor, or family members.

Discovering templates are very handy, especially for new advisors. The templates save you the embarrassment of phoning the client a number of times after an initial meeting to get information that you forgot to ask for the first time.

While I am a supporter of the discovering document, it does also have a few significant drawbacks that are important for you to know. For instance, imagine this scenario:

You are sitting in front of your family physician to talk about a medical concern. The doctor takes out his four-page discovering document and proceeds to ask you a number of questions, most of which have no relation at all to your immediate concern. Regardless, he carefully and meticulously goes through each question.

How would you feel? Would you be comfortable with the doctor? Would you want your children and other loved ones to place their future health in his hands? Have you ever seen a medical doctor do that?

No, they don't—because they are trusted professionals.

In the insurance and financial services field, we are financial "doctors". What I prefer to a discovering document is just a blank legal pad. I read the discovering document and convert it into a mind map. I study the mind map and then follow it in my head.

In the beginning, I used to write little letters in the margin of the legal pad to guide me through the mind map. This created a more professional appearance in the client's eyes.

A few years ago, I realized I was underestimating the power of a mind map. The most analytical and cautious client I have ever met arrived at my office with a roughly fifty-page financial plan, drawn up for him by an obviously skilled and highly experienced advisor. As I perused his plan, I realized that I would have to do something completely different if I wanted to win this client over.

We sat down in my boardroom, where I have a number of big windows. I used coloured whiteboard markers to draw a mind map of the client's financial situation on the glass. The plan was extensive, taking up three glass panels. After about three hours of discussions, the mind map looked like an explosion. Only the three of us (his wife was also present) could have understood what it meant. It would have been complete gibberish for anybody else.

I will never forget his closing remark: "So you want me to choose between this (holding the financial plan in his hand) or that on the glass?"

Almost ashamedly, I said, "Yes."

"I choose the glass," he replied.

That gained a wonderful client for me, and it also opened my eyes to the power of mind maps.

I now take A3 paper with me when I see clients. I spread it out in front of the client. We start at the top left corner with a stick figure of him and his wife and kids. We sketch out their marital regime, house, business, and so on. It is remarkable how the clients understand the mind map and how they will often start drawing on the map themselves. They almost always ask for the map when we are done, so I take a photo to put in the file and give the client the map.

This initial sketch is, of course, afterwards formalized in a full financial needs analysis and implementation of the agreed-upon financial plan.

Here is an example of one I did with a client recently. See if you can figure out what we discussed.

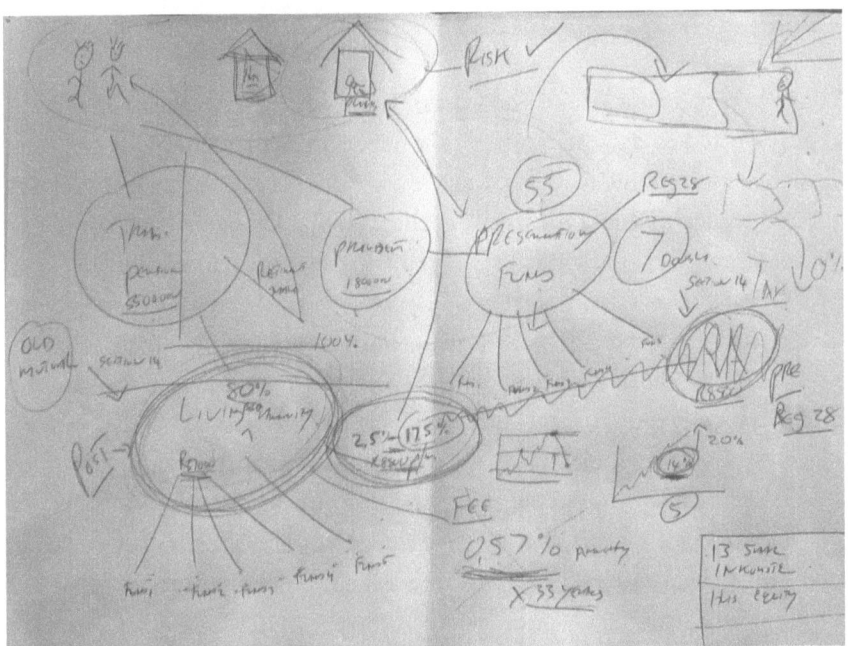

The Uncomfortable Silence

After proposing a solution to the client, there is often a period of silence in the room while the client processes all of the information. This silence can feel quite uncomfortable. The golden rule, according to traditional sales training, is not to interrupt this quiet time, as "he who speaks first loses".

The reality is that this silence is only uncomfortable for a person who is pitching a sale. In this situation, when the client becomes quiet, allow all the time the client needs to process the information you just gave, and to work out whether to accept your offer.

If you interrupt the client during this stage in the process, you will also interrupt the client's overall chain of thought. Then it is much more likely that the default reaction will be to tell you no or, at the very least, to defer an answer until a later time. The silence is not uncomfortable for client; they are at work in another part of their brain. By all means, allow their brain to process it all before moving on to the next part of your agenda.

Taking the Next Logical Step

When getting close to the part of the meeting with the client that is often referred to as "the closing", the successful trusted advisor does not actually close a client at all. If you have conducted the meeting by following the proper techniques, you and the client will collectively have come to a solution, and the next logical step is to complete the paperwork.

When this occurs, not only will you be considered an expert advisor rather than a salesperson by the client, but you will also be likely to retain policies from year to year, because the client has helped to find the solution and is typically quite happy with the outcome. It is your job as the advisor to gently and respectfully lead your clients towards solutions. You must lead! (More on this in chapter 10, "The Prophet of Doom".)

Through all of this, always be mindful of the six steps of financial planning. These must all be addressed in some way or another:

1. Establish and define the relationship with the client.
2. Collect the client's information.
3. Analyse and assess the client's financial situation.
4. Develop the client's financial plan and present it to the client.
5. Implement the financial plan's recommendations.
6. Review the client's situation at least annually.

A Different Kind of Call

In many ways, success in sales boils down to being respectful and courteous to the client. Providing solutions to your clients' needs should never be about just randomly picking a policy and then forcing a client to buy, regardless of the client's actual requirements.

Rather, when you work in conjunction with your client—beginning by ensuring that you and the client are a good fit—it is much more likely that you will create a book of business that is filled with your ideal customers. Likewise, the client will feel that they have secured a trusted advisor for the long term.

***

Success Action Steps

Moving away from the traditional ways of securing clients can initially seem difficult. This is particularly the case if you have been in a sales-related position for many years. While building relationships may take a bit longer to achieve, doing so can have numerous long-term rewards for both you and your clients.

Come up with a list of key questions to ask your clients that can help you and them to better narrow down their needs. Then come to agreeable, collective solutions as a team. For examples of discovering templates and mind maps, go to www.andreroos.com.

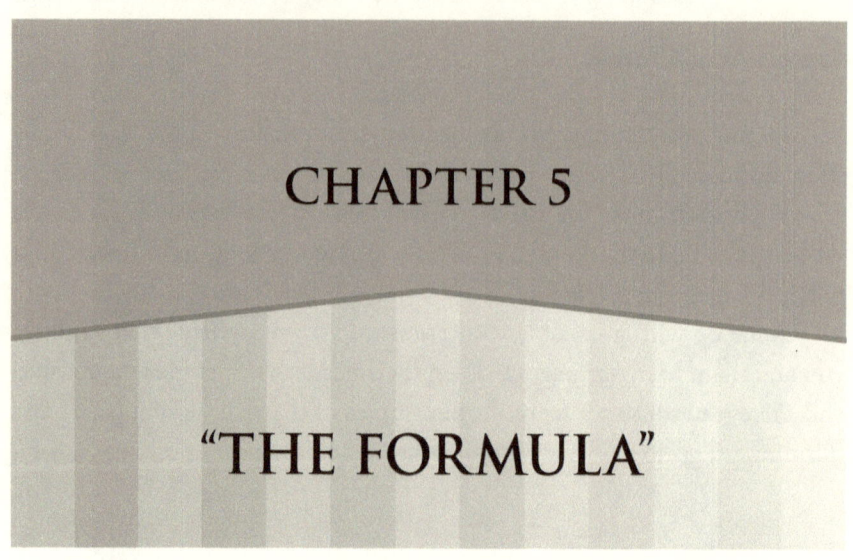

CHAPTER 5

"THE FORMULA"

Everything must be made as simple as possible. But not simpler.

—Albert Einstein

We all go through difficult periods at one time or another. These could be due to the death of a loved one, divorce, loss of a job, or a natural disaster, to name just a few possibilities.

While these incidents can certainly be rough to endure, it is how we handle such situations that can leave a nasty, long-lasting scar or that can provide us with the courage and motivation to keep moving forward.

Making It through to the Other Side, One Positive Incident at a Time

Just a few years ago, I went through a devastating period. What saved me was the realization that today is all we have. Yesterday is gone, and tomorrow is uncertain. So we must make the most of what we have right now.

With that in mind, I told myself not to worry about tomorrow, as each day already has enough worries of its own (Matthew 6:34). If we spend too much of our time worrying about tomorrow and the future, then it will surely steal our present.

If it is true that time heals all wounds, then focusing on day-to-day living can be an excellent first step to getting through the rough times in your life. In my case, each day when I awoke, I asked myself several pertinent questions:

- Do I have enough food for today? (Yes)

- Will I have a bed to sleep in tonight? (Again, yes)

- Will my car or my home be repossessed today? (No!)

Given my answers, I knew that I should be thankful. I was far ahead of many other people in this world. I was also acutely aware that my most basic of physiological needs were being met, according to the late scientist Abraham Maslow.

Maslow set out to prove that humans are motivated to achieve fulfilment of certain needs, and that some of these needs take precedence over others. For example, our most basic need is for physical survival, which in turn is the first thing that motivates our human behaviour to attain food, shelter, and clothing. Once that level of need is fulfilled, then the next level up becomes what motivates us, and so on.[1]

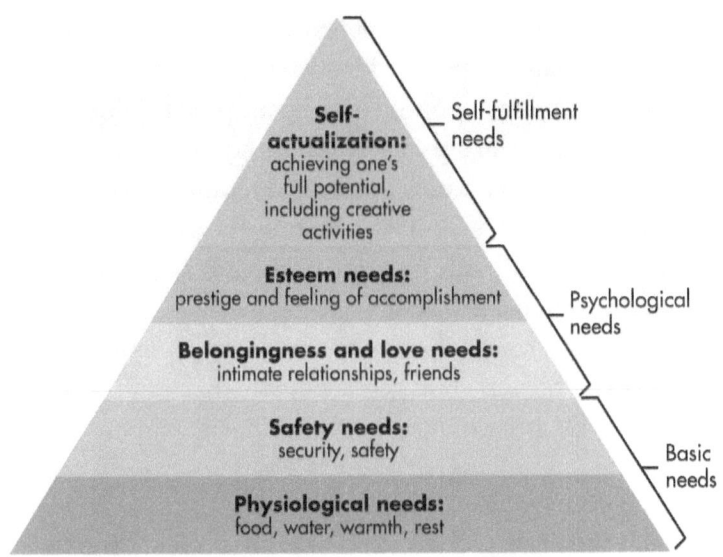

Maslow's hierarchy of needs. Source: *Simply Psychology*.

In Maslow's hierarchy of needs, the pyramid base—as well as the next three levels up—are referred to as "deficiency needs". When such needs are unmet, they are said to motivate people. The longer these needs go unmet, the stronger the need to fulfil them becomes.

The truth is that every human is capable of and has the desire to move up this hierarchy of needs towards a level of self-actualization. Unfortunately, the progress we make can often be disrupted by failure to meet the lower-level needs. Life experiences such as divorce or job loss can cause an individual to fluctuate between levels of the hierarchy.[2]

In addition to asking and answering the questions regarding meeting my basic needs, I took things one step further in order to keep myself motivated and help ensure that I was truly making progress towards my goals. I asked, "What one positive thing can I do today that will lead me closer to my goals?"

Just one!

And then I did it.

How to Get a Running Start

One of the best ways to get and remain ahead of the pack is to start your day early. Although you may not currently consider yourself to be a morning person, changing your waking habit can be extremely beneficial. This is the case both in your business and your personal life.

For example, according to Hal Elrod, author of *The Miracle Morning* book series, "How you start each morning determines your mindset, and the context, for the rest of your day. Start every day with a purposeful, disciplined, growth-infused, and goal-oriented morning, and you're virtually guaranteed to crush your day."[5]

Elrod goes on to say that the more you dig into mornings, the more the proof mounts that the early bird gets a lot more than just the worm. Here are a few advantages to starting your day with vigour, purpose, and routine:

- You'll be more proactive.
- You'll anticipate problems and head them off at the pass.
- You'll have more energy.

- You'll gain early bird advantages and avoid night owl disadvantages.
- You'll plan like a pro.[3]

Regarding planning, he adds, "Morning folks have the time to organize, anticipate, and plan for their day. Our sleepy counterparts are reactive rather than proactive, leaving a lot to chance."[4]

Having a regular, healthy morning ritual can produce other benefits. For instance, it can help you filter out the negative forces in your life and have a keener focus on the positive.

There are a number of items that you can get checked off your daily list long before you even enter the office. In so doing, you will be better able to begin your work day invigorated.

- reading
- exercising
- visualizing
- planning
- eating a healthy breakfast

Although you may not ever have thought about it in this context, you are the machine that creates where you are going. An insurance or financial advisor can be an extremely positive force in your clients' lives, helping them to create wealth, leave a legacy, and protect the people and things that are important to them.

Creating the Formula for Success

Once you have completed your morning ritual and get to the office, the formula—*your* formula—begins. For many years, the sales formula has been all about generating activity, which is expected to produce certain results.

That formula mostly consisted of the following (per week):

- make one hundred calls
- get fifteen first-time appointments

- see ten people (some of your appointments will cancel)
- complete seven financial needs analyses
- propose solutions to five people
- close three sales
- get five referrals per client

While you will likely make some adjustments to this process over time, based on what works best for you, this success formula can be broken down into its most critical components, without which it will not work.

Begin with your commitment to being a trusted financial advisor. You must be committed and have a clear idea of where you're going (e.g., the results that you aim to produce, the type of client you wish to work with), as these are keys to keeping your motivation on track. The formula describes the activities that you need to do in order to generate the appropriate number of prospects that will get you to 120 clients in the shortest period of time.

Let's break down the success formula in more detail.

You Are Committed

The first component of the formula—and according to many, the most important factor—is to be committed. Fully committed!

You truly want to be a trusted financial advisor. Your aim is to work with just 120 clients. Not five hundred or a thousand. Just 120.

It is a well-known and documented fact that the failure rate of financial advisors is very high. This means that a large percentage of advisors who are currently in the industry will not be around in five years' time. What are some of the reasons for that?

In some cases, an individual may dabble in finance to see whether the job is suitable for them. They are merely trying it out. Others may find the prospecting part of the business too challenging. Some fail due to their fear of rejection or the fluctuating income. Others are simply not cut out for the industry. Whatever the reasons, many advisors do not make it.

But is that fair to their clients? Likewise, for wannabe advisors supporting a family, is this fair to them?

If you are serious, committed professional, you don't necessarily need to be the best of the best. You do need to be dedicated to serving your clients and meeting your goals. Your competitive focus is to "outrun" other advisors.

This can be summed up in a story. Consider two friends who are planning to go hiking in the woods. In these woods, there is a chance that the hikers will run into hungry bears. This could be quite detrimental, to say the least!

So, for several weeks prior to the hike, one of the friends regularly runs long distances to train for the event. His hiking partner ask why he is training so hard. After all, there is no way that a human could outrun a bear. The first young man responds, "I don't need to outrun the bears. I only need to outrun *you*!"

My personal experience is that most advisors fail simply because they quit to soon. Push through, not just for yourself but for the sake of the clients who trusted you!

You Need to Know Where You Are Going

The next step in your formula is that you need to know where you are going. Remember, everyone in the world is not your client. Unfortunately, most newer advisors in particular have no clear-cut vision, so they end up going into crisis mode. At that point, the advisor appears to be desperate—and nobody wants to buy from a desperate salesperson. This is about as far away as you can get from achieving your ultimate goal of being a trusted advisor.

Rather, you should always be in adventure mode. In this industry, we never know what is coming our way. For example, while you may be going through a sales slump right now, it could be that the very next phone call will gain you your best client ever, and that client might be a person of influence, and it could change your entire career. Just a single call!

Therefore, it is essential to keep in mind that opportunity knocks very quickly. If you don't open the door, it will be gone.

It is easier to know where you want to go if you take the time to visualize it: the type of life you want to live, the type of home you want to live in, the type of clients you want to serve, and the level of success that you ultimately want to achieve. Visualization can be helped along by knowing the type of clients that you *do not* wish to have.

Think about it as a map of the place you want to go. Map in mind, you will find ways to get there—and you will keep moving forward until you arrive.

But the old ways of selling will not typically get anyone to their ultimate destination. In fact, there are many ways that the old-school ways of selling can actually sabotage your sales career. For instance, many traditional sales methods recommend that you call on your family and friends. In other words, contact your warm market first, and then branch out from there. But I believe there is a substantial problem with this way of thinking.

First, your family and friends may not be the type of clients you wish to work with. If your target client is a pilot who earns a certain income, how likely is it that your friends and family members just happen to fit this mould? Unless they do, they are not the best people for you to prospect.

A better plan of action is to contact your targets directly. Go where the fish already are. When targeting those who are successful, conduct yourself in a manner that appeals to them. Those who are successful want to work with advisors who are also successful.

How can you accomplish this?

One way is by letting prospects know that you only have limited space on your client list. As mentioned previously, this creates an issue of supply and demand. Another way is to look the part, dressing like you're already successful.

Napoleon Hill, author of the timeless book *Think and Grow Rich*, also wrote a compelling piece titled Dress for Success: The Psychology of Good Clothes. Hill states that "wearing good clothes signals others that you are already prosperous and successful, and it also gives you more self-confidence, and it enables you to succeed".[6]

Likewise, you need to put yourself where other successful people already are. If you are spending time with those who do not earn much money, then you are not likely to cultivate clients who are well off. By spending time with those who are in your target market, you will be much more likely to obtain more well-off clients. Once you've gotten started, the momentum will pick up steam. Remember, success breeds success!

Schedule Your Time—Starting with Marketing

Even if you are committed to being a trusted advisor, and even if you know where you want to go, there is another thing you'll need in order to be successful, and that is people to talk to.

To gather those people, the next component of the formula involves setting aside a certain, specific amount of time to market your services. You should ideally schedule at least three hours per day for marketing, and these should be the first hours of the workday, when you are apt to have the most energy and motivation. You can set up in-person meetings with prospects and clients for later that same afternoon. If you are able to see between twelve and fifteen people per week, be it first appointments, second appointments or even third appointments you should easily be able to have 120 clients in place within a year.

It is absolutely essential that you plan your day and your business. Otherwise, your day and your business will run you, and that can easily lead to chaos, frustration, and stress.

So what is the best method to go about your marketing? Calling prospects on the phone.

Most people who make their living in sales are not at all fond of the telephone. In fact, many will find any reason on earth not to use the telephone to call potential clients. This, however, can be a big mistake.

While *only* using the telephone to generate clients can be somewhat of a gamble, doing so as part of your overall marketing plan can allow you to reach out to a large number of prospects in a short period of time.

In some ways, making phone calls to prospects is like playing roulette. You do not know what state of mind the prospect is in when they answer the phone. They could be in a good or a bad mood. They could be going through a difficult time. Alternatively, they could have just received a lucrative promotion at work and be feeling great. In most cases, though, it is not likely that the prospect is thinking about insurance.

So with this in mind, do not become discouraged. You may just find someone who is in that right frame of mind and is willing to set an appointment to meet with you.

The quotation at the start of this chapter, from Albert Einstein, praises simplicity. Another Einstein observation is relevant to following through with the phoning part of your formula: "When the number of factors coming into play in a phenomenological complex is too large, scientific method in most cases fails. One need only think of the weather, in which case the prediction even for a few days ahead is impossible."[7]

In addition to contacting potential clients directly, there is also a way to set up a system that eventually will generate for you a constant flow of good, solid referrals. That is by contacting those who are considered centres of influence.

Most people will rely on various professionals in their lives. These usually include individuals from the following specialities:

- law
- accounting
- medicine
- faith
- finance

While these professionals are all important, just one cannot provide all of the advice that a person needs. It can make sense for you as a sales professional to align yourself with other professionals, so that when their clients need an insurance advisor, those professionals will think to refer you.

It can take time to work your way into networks of professionals. However, once you create a system of generating referrals through these networks, the system will become self-perpetuating.

Regardless of whether you are contacting professionals, centres of influence, or individual consumers, when you are in the midst of your phoning sessions, it is imperative that you remain focused on that activity alone. This is why you should plan your marketing time in advance and place it on your schedule. This as an activity that must be done—and done for a minimum of three hours per workday. Activities that are included in your schedule typically get done. Items that are not in your schedule typically don't.

The Many Advantages of Having a Formula in Place

The beauty of having a formula is that you have specific steps to go through that will help you reach your goals. It's like having a recipe to follow. It provides you with step-by-step instructions so you know exactly what you need to be doing next.

Think about how a recipe works. They make it easier to attain a certain outcome by giving you a series of tasks in proper order. And, because a dish can taste different to different people, most recipes leave room for a bit of tweaking. As you work your way through your activity recipe, it is important that you track your progress in order to determine what works and what does not. Then make the necessary adjustments to your formula.

Having a good, solid recipe in place can help to get you through anything—even the worst of times. That's because you'll know exactly what you need to do each day, from the moment you wake up.

Recipes help to keep you going when you get discouraged. They help you to plant seeds now that can be harvested later. Think of it like this: there is a season for everything in life. The bad times will not last forever. But you have to continue on your path in order to get through.

Just as farmers have seasons for planting and harvesting, financial advisors have seasons for prospecting (planting the seeds), and fulfilment (getting yourself up to 120 clients). Success in each endeavour requires a plan. You can pick up momentum by sticking to your recipe and by doing a positive thing each day that moves you towards your goals.

My Own Formula

A few weeks ago, in one of my advisor meetings I asked an advisor to tell the group about her formula, her daily means of operation.

She said, "I wake up at 6 a.m. I do Bible study and prayer for about thirty minutes. I prepare breakfast and then leave for the office at around 8 a.m. Then I do prospecting and telephoning till about 11 a.m. From 11 a.m. on, I see my clients. I go to bed at about 10 p.m."

Could you follow her recipe for success?

In terms of detail, this is the same as saying, "Take flour, sugar, and cocoa. Mix them in a bowl and put the batter in the oven." Would that give you a chocolate cake? Nope. About all it is likely to give you is a bowl that blows up and a seriously angry spouse. Too many crucial details are missing.

Your daily means of operation (DMO) should be as detailed and custom made for you as possible. It is always—yes, always—a work in progress, so it needs to be updated and expanded until it works for you. This means that it will change as your career and life change.

Life is not something that only happens to your clients. It happens to you as well, and as life changes, your DMO should adapt. How do you know if your DMO works? Simple—it produces results for you!

Here is my current DMO as an example. You will notice that personal energy management forms part of my formula.

I rise around 5 a.m. The alarm clock is placed on the far side of the bedroom, to force me to get up immediately with no snoozing. I drink a full glass of cold water to rehydrate from the hours that my body was asleep. (We dehydrate during the night). I follow it with a cup of tea.

Then I start my miracle morning routine, from the book *Miracle Morning* by Hal Elrod:

- ten minutes of prayer
- five minutes of silence
- five minutes of visualizing my objectives
- five minutes of personal affirmations

Yes, I know the affirmations sound corny, but they really work. The world does a stern job in telling us where we fall short. A daily affirmation reminds you of who you really are.

Then I go for a walk or cycle to get the blood flowing and the heart rate up. I've also experimented with cryotherapy, ice pools, and saunas to kick-start my body and mind. All of these work very well.

I have a half-hour drive to work. I fill that time with an audio book, using Audacity. I don't see the point of listening to some radio DJ talking nonsense, or even worse, listening to the news. That will usually start your day off on a poor note. I try not to burden myself with matters that are out of my direct control. On average I listen to one hundred and twenty books a year by utilizing my drive time.

I believe in some alone time, or me time, before work. There is a wonderful coffee shop surrounded by vineyards that I visit every morning. The food is good and the coffee is excellent. I spend about forty-five minutes in the coffee shop, brainstorming on a paper notepad. I plan my day and write down important things for myself. Whatever comes up, I write it down. This very book was birthed in that coffee shop.

After breakfast, I start my thirty-point day. This is a simple system that I found on a piece of paper in a vacated office when I started in the industry. It originally was a twenty-five-point system, but I tweaked it for myself, and it became a thirty-point system.

Every income-producing activity is given a weight. The more profitable the activity is, the higher the weight that is assigned to it. Training and company meetings have a fifteen-point weight, which means that even if my day is fully scheduled with training, I still need to find the time to earn at least fifteen more points.

The rule is simple: I don't go to bed until I have thirty points. I record my points on my production board (more about that later).

I avoid seeing clients in the evenings as much as possible. I prefer to spend my evenings with my wife and family. However, note that in the beginning of your career, you do what you have to do, and seeing clients in the evening is hard to avoid.

Before bedtime, I take a long, warm bath and add essential oils to assist my sleeping. I drink a glass of ice water in the bath, again for hydration. I eat six to ten almonds to keep my blood sugar up during the night.

I then take a few minutes to plan the next day. Finally, I do some fiction reading on my Kindle for about five minutes, if I am lucky, before I fall asleep.

I know it sounds extensive, but it works for me. Of course, I don't always stick to it completely.

I have a month-end ritual as well that I feel is worth mentioning. I remind my advisors of this every month. On the first day of the month, I do the following:

- call all my clients of the previous month as a follow-up, and also as a reminder of when they will hear from me again
- clear my inbox
- clean my desk
- clean my car
- clean my production board and fill in the targets for the new month
- thank my support staff for the previous month

I see this as my clean start for the new month. It normally takes only a morning to complete. Then I take the afternoon off to do something fun and relaxing. This helps immensely to clear my head going forward.

Momentum

By definition, the Merriam Webster dictionary states that momentum is "the quantity of motion of a moving body, measured as a product of mass and velocity". The most important thing in any business is to create momentum. Years ago, I learned this from a former business partner. He taught me how to measure momentum in one's business.

The only way to measure business momentum is by the number of times the phone rings. That's it! Sounds simple, doesn't it? Count the calls as you start your practice and for as long as your phone is not ringing often enough to interrupt you, you have no momentum in your business.

To get people to phone you is harder than you might think. I will never forget when I had phone lines installed at my previous company. Nobody knew the number, and the phones were eerily silent. Five years later, I was sitting in my upstairs office, listening to the phones ringing non-stop. I couldn't help but remind myself of how hard it had been and what I'd had to endure just to get those phones ringing.

I explain a new financial services practice like this to my new advisor trainees: it is like a snowball. Currently, you have a little snowball in front of you and it is going nowhere (i.e., the phone is dead silent). Every single day, you need to push this little snowball. It will get bigger day by day, provided of course that you keep on pushing it.

Until your business grows, the ball will stop dead the moment you stop pushing it. Then one day you will briefly stop pushing it, and lo and behold, the ball does not stop immediately. It rolls on for a few metres on its own. A while later when you stop, the ball keeps on going, albeit slowly. As you help it along, it speeds up. Eventually it is almost rolling away from you. You need to run to keep up with it. Your consistent and dedicated hard work to get the ball rolling is now paying off hugely.

The thirty-point daily plan will be your biggest asset in building this momentum.

I stopped pushing the snowball three years ago when I took on my new role as a business principal and advisor coach. I have not made a single phone call to a prospect in three years. In fact, I have done absolutely nothing proactively to gain business. I have only processed what has come my way when the phone rings.

The first year, the ball kept on rolling under the momentum of my record in previous employment. The second year, the ball showed no sign of slowing down. At the beginning of the third year, I reassigned four hundred and twenty of my clients to other advisors to get my book down to around eighty of my best clients, based upon my relationship with them. This did a little bit of damage to the momentum, but far less than I expected.

On its current trajectory, the ball is likely to take another two to three years to slow down to a walking pace. Note that as long as I remain in the industry, the ball will never stop rolling completely. That is the beauty of momentum.

In the beginning days of building my practice, I found that one of the rules of momentum is this: lose one, lose three. In other words, lose one hour of pushing and you will lose three hours of momentum. Lose one whole day of pushing, and you lose three days of momentum. And so on.

The Psychology of the Production Board

A few years ago, I was studying the power of the subconscious mind. Most of it I didn't really understand, bar that the subconscious mind is extremely powerful and we still know very little about it.

I experimented with giving my subconscious mind some problems to resolve. To do so, I meditated on the problem before going to bed. Studies showed that the subconscious mind would work on the problem during the night and supposedly provide you with a solution in the morning.

Did it work? Sometimes it did; sometimes it didn't. Regardless, I learned enough to incorporate it into my business via my production board.

What exactly is a production board? It is a big whiteboard that is the last thing I see before I go to bed and the first thing I see when I wake up. My wife hated it when I installed it, but she liked the fruits it produced.

On this board, I draw five blocks at the top to record my daily thirty-point score. My production targets are prominent. There is a list of confirmed business for the month in one column, and a list of pipeline, or potential business, in another column.

Seeing this board every single night before bed and every single morning when I wake up has done something to me and my subconscious mind. It is hard to explain, but when the board looks good, I sleep differently. This board is a constant reminder, right there in my bedroom, of my need to do something to create momentum and achieve my goals.

A big whiteboard is good, but even a mirror will do. Don't fool yourself by creating a small chart on your tablet or smartphone. Create a big one and make sure that the important people in your life know how to read it.

Tying It All Together

Getting from one point to another typically takes focus and a plan. The good news is that your plan or recipe for success does not have to be complicated. It just requires that you get and stay on track using a formula—ideally a formula that is aligned with what works for you.

What will you do when you wake up tomorrow morning?

Once you have your formula in place, you will know. Your success formula will soon turn into a habit and you will be on your way to putting the system in motion for your success.

***

Success Action Steps

To better ensure success with meeting prospects and identifying the ones who will become part of your 120-client mix, you need to have a plan in place for what you will do with your time each day. In other words, you need a formula.

Take some time now and develop your formula. Keep in mind that it doesn't need to be perfect yet. You can make changes over time to help it work better for you. But it does need to provide you with a step-by-step, actionable recipe that you can implement as soon as you open your eyes each day.

In addition, be sure that you install a production board. This is a key component to seeing your goals, and thereby achieving them!

Go to www.andreroos.com to download my thirty-point plan spreadsheet, as well as a production board layout. These items will be extremely beneficial in getting you closer to your ultimate production goals.

CHAPTER 6

THE FIVE PROFESSIONALS

Many receive advice, only the wise profit from it.

—Harper Lee

Receiving good advice is a central component to anyone's effective decision-making. In many cases, receiving guidance is considered "the passive consumption of wisdom".[1] It can lead individuals to move forward with good judgement.

When an exchange of advice is done well, those on either side of the table can benefit. For example, those who receive such guidance can move forward with developing and implementing better solutions to problems than they otherwise would have devised on their own. Further, good advice can add texture and nuance to their overall thinking—so much so that studies have shown that well-guided individuals can overcome cognitive biases, as well as other possible flaws in their logic.

In turn, advisors who are able to acutely listen to their clients can learn a great deal from the issues that are brought to them. On top of that, the rule of reciprocity can be an extremely powerful force, in that offering good advice will often create a debt of sorts that the recipient of the advice will willingly want to repay. In the case of a client/financial advisor relationship, repayment could come in the form of freely offering referrals, doing additional business with the advisor, and remaining with the advisor for an extended period of time.

The Journey to a Successful Life Is Not a Solitary Road

Unless you are locked away on a deserted island, it is safe to say that there are other people in your life with whom you interact. In some cases, the interaction may be on a regular, even daily basis. In other instances, interaction may occur only periodically.

Some of these people play a key role in your journey towards success. You may not always realize just how important they are.

Consider the avid mountaineer who has a goal of climbing Mount Everest. The climber may be credited with accomplishing this task, but it could not be accomplished without the help of others along the way. These can include a guide, an equipment advisor, and trainers and colleagues from prior climbs. Crucial support may also include words of encouragement from people in the climber's life who have never climbed themselves.

No one truly reaches the summit alone. There is always somebody climbing with you. Some of them are people who are closest to you, such as family members and friends. Others are on a professional level, guiding you towards professional goals on a variety of levels.

I believe that each person who takes life seriously must have professionals from at least five specialities in their life:

- law
- accounting
- medicine
- faith
- finance

This is the case for your clients, for other advisors, and for the professionals themselves. Often, financial advisors will not only have medical, accounting, legal, and spiritual professionals in their lives, but also their own financial advisors. This makes sense, as it can be extremely beneficial to have another professional in the field to give you their perspective on your financial plan. Consider that those in the medical profession have their own doctors, as they cannot logically diagnose each and every one of their ailments themselves.

As an advisor, you work hard to develop yourself, not just mentally by learning new and unique ways to assist your clients with their money, but also physically, legally, spiritually, and psychologically. Each of these professionals plays a specific role in your and your clients' overall development.

For example, it goes without saying that having someone guide you with advice for attaining and maintaining optimal health can be priceless. While we all know that eating right, exercising, and getting regular health check-ups are important, if an issue comes along, it is pertinent to have a trained medical professional take a closer look so that it can be diagnosed and properly treated.

An accountant is also an essential advisor. This is the case whether you use a tax professional for personal reasons only, or if you are a business owner.

Another key professional advisor is an attorney. There is an endless array of potential legal issues that one can become involved in, personally, professionally, or both, and nobody knows when an issue may occur. Having an established relationship with a legal professional is essential.

Many people rely on spiritual advice from a rabbi, priest, pastor, or other religious professional. This can be highly beneficial to you in finding direction and peace, as well as in allowing a higher power to guide you.

Financial advice is likewise key to attaining overall success. Consumers and business owners need financial advice to help them reach their goals.

There are also other types of advice that can assist you as well. For example, many people can benefit from working with a life coach, a psychologist, or a mentor.

It is important to note that success follows happiness and self-confidence, not the other way around. One does not become successful and then, suddenly, happy, self-confident, and fulfilled. Rather, those who are already happy and who have confidence in themselves will become successful.

If understood and applied correctly, the *fivepro concept* (which is short for "five professionals") eliminates the need to make hundreds of phone calls per day. In essence, you act as a relationship broker between your client and the five professionals—of which you, of course, are one.

Much has been written over the years about what motivates people.

We all know that money is not even in the top five. The important drivers include the following:

- safety
- comfort
- love
- pleasure
- recognition

I believe that one of the strongest motivational factors is *results*. I believe that all people are motivated by results much more so than they are by money. Potentially great financial advisors have walked away from this amazing career because of a lack of results from doing what they were taught to do.

Here is a short, hypothetical example of how I would use the fivepro concept to build a book of clients if I had just started out as an advisor in a new town. No one would know that I was brand-new in town and did not already have a book of clients.

Day One: I would phone up a few attorneys, explaining who I am and that I am looking for an attorney to refer my clients to. I would ask to set up appointments to briefly discuss this with each attorney. I would do the same with members of the other professional categories.

This concept works very well with most professionals except doctors. People obviously don't need a referral from a financial advisor to find a doctor. To connect with doctors, I use other techniques.

A number of years ago, I used the referral approach as a rationale to test drive all the new Aston Martin sports vehicles. I was invited to all the local dealers' social events and launches, and of course met many Aston Martin owners. This not only helped me find successful clients, but also allowed me to get behind the wheel of some fantastic vehicles!

When I meet with an attorney, I explain the fivepro concept and specifically ask about their capacity for new relationships. I explain that my clients are ambitious individuals, often entrepreneurs or other business leaders, and they will almost certainly be in need of a good attorney. I also explain that some might not have an immediate need, but would like to have a relationship with a good attorney for future purposes. I ask if the attorney is willing to have quick coffee meeting with a client at a convenient time for him. These are introductory meetings for which the attorney does not charge.

The attorney might reply that they only have capacity for ten such relationships. I am very happy with that and promise to arrange ten such meetings. Before I conclude, I ask him who his own professionals are and if he would mind referring me to them. A snowball is born.

If my luck is in, the attorney might not have all the professionals they need, and I can offer to arrange introductions. If the attorney has no financial advisor, then I have hit the jackpot. I politely ask if they would like me to act as advisor. The law of reciprocation kicks in, and the snowball starts to move.

If, as sometimes happens, the meeting falls flat, I simply move on to the next attorney.

If the attorney refers me to other professionals, such as an accountant, I will phone the accountant, say that the attorney referred me, and set up an appointment. The process starts over again. Sooner or later, I will have a meeting with an entrepreneur or ambitious individual who is not among the five professionals. By that time I will already have a network of professionals I can introduce that individual to.

If the businessperson does not have an attorney, that will be my first promised introduction to the attorney I originally met with. The ten promised meetings are now down to nine. Working this way, I will make good on my promise of ten meetings within weeks.

With doctors, I use a more traditional approach. I call the doctor, mention who referred me, and explain what value I can bring to the doctor's personal finances as well as the medical practice. I meet the doctor, discuss the financial planning, explain the fivepro concept, and move on. If the doctor already has professionals in place, I ask to meet them. If not, I introduce the doctor to my network.

Using this model, I believe it is possible to build at least twenty client relationships within three months, all without making a single prospecting cold call. People are far more likely to meet with you if you bring them something they can benefit from. Remember, they don't know what you have. You might be representing some of the wealthiest people in the country, as the manager of Aston Martin thought—they don't know.

Again, the law of reciprocation works in your favour.

Who Fits the Five Professionals Concept?

Even if you plan to keep your total client list at 120, each client will likely be very different from the others. Likewise, your clients will likely exhibit varying levels of success. This could be due in part to what stage they are in in their lives. For instance, are they just starting their careers? Or are they middle-aged and taking on the task of starting their own business? Or are they nearing retirement?

Success can mean different things to different people. One person may feel that success has to do primarily with ensuring good health. That person may work diligently to eat the right foods, take part in regular exercise, and get an ample amount of sleep every night.

Other people may feel that true success has to do with building up a large net worth. They are constantly learning about various investment opportunities, and taking part in those that make sense to them.

In every case, people want to better their lives. Regardless of what your client thinks exemplifies success, you must let every client know that you are committed to *all* of them. You are committed to their ongoing growth and their journey towards achieving their goals.

In order to provide your clients with the very best service and advice, as well as to work most cohesively with your clients' other advisors, you must truly listen to what your clients say about their lives, their goals, their dreams, and their needs.

By explaining to your clients and ensuring that they fully understand the concept of the five professionals, you will be able to say to them with conviction, "I am committed to your development and your success."

It is absolutely essential that your client have ambition in order to fit in with the five professionals concept. The only person who really does not fit the model is the person who does not have ambition in any area.

Andre Roos

How to Cultivate Relationships with Your Clients' Other Professionals

Pursuing relationships with your clients' other professionals can be highly beneficial for them and for you. For them, having all of their primary professionals working together better ensures that all of the key components in their lives are aligned. For you, developing relationships with professionals who are not competitors provides an ideal way of mutually referring clients without having to ask for referrals. It can eventually allow you to step away from "dialling for dollars" on the telephone every day, trying to build up your business.

In cultivating relationships with your clients' other professionals, it is important to follow certain steps. Begin by asking your clients if they currently have an attorney, an accountant, and so on. If a client answers yes, then ask about their relationships with these professionals. For instance, is the relationship good and beneficial? It can be helpful if you also inquire as to whether the other professionals are relational and provide true benefits to your client, or if they are more transactional and really only interested in making a sale to your client.

If the relationship is transactional, the next step is to ask your client if they would like to be introduced to a new professional in that category. If the client has a good, relational relationship with their other professionals, ask your client to introduce you to them. In making these requests, you should explain to your client the many benefits of having their professionals working together. Chief among these benefits is that professional cooperation can help to ensure that planning gaps are filled in, and that nothing important in the client's life is falling through the proverbial cracks.

Once you have been introduced to the clients' other key professionals and have built relationships with them, you will be in a much better position to give and receive referrals with these individuals.

It is important to keep in mind that these new relationships may not immediately translate into new business. When that happens will depend upon the needs of a given advisor's clients. However, when a need does arise, a professional in your network will be much more apt to contact you.

A short animated video explaining the fivepro concept, is available on my website, www.anderoos.com.

***

Success Action Steps

Using the fivepro concept can be life-changing. This is true for your clients as well as for your own personal development. Not only can this concept enhance the relationships you have with your clients, but it can also allow you to move away from the old way of generating business on the phone. It could in fact mean that you'll never need to play telephone roulette again to generate new clients.

Take some time to do the following two activities. First, write down who your personal five professionals are. Include advisors in the areas of:

1. Medical:_____
2. Accounting:_____
3. Legal:_____
4. Spiritual:_____
5. Financial:_____

Next, write down at least five points on how and why the concept of the five professionals provides so much value. This will help you to key in on certain points when explaining this concept to your clients and prospects.

1. _____
2. _____
3. _____
4. _____
5. _____

CHAPTER 7

NURTURE YOUR INVESTMENT

Make the customer the hero of your story.

—Ann Handley

As a financial advisor, you can have the most exquisite office space, endless education about properly structure savings and income plans, and a long list of professional designations following your name on your business card. But without clients, you'll be out of business. Period.

Advisors don't typically put a monetary value on their clients or see their clients as "investments" or "assets". Because of that, many advisors end up neglecting their clients, thereby earning a poor return on what are, in fact, assets.

Clients Are Your Financial Services Practice's Assets

Customers are literally the lifeblood of any organization. Without them, your business would have no revenue, no profit, and no income for you. Building and fostering an environment in which clients feel loyal to you and your business is a very wise investment in your future.

For the most part, people enjoy doing business with other people, especially if a professional truly listen to client needs and makes the client feel like they are more than just the next commission check. Therefore, it is essential for insurance and financial advisors to focus on creating client relationships, not just to go through the motions of transacting product sales.

Most clients respond favourably to genuine interactions with their advisors. As they do, the relationship will grow. With that in mind, it makes sense to think of your customers as investments or assets. Nurture those investments over time.

What Is Your Customer Acquisition Cost and Value?

In any business, there is a cost of acquiring customers, as well as a customer value. Cost and value can vary a great deal from one industry to another, and even from one financial advisor to another. It is important to keep in mind that the cost of acquiring a client needs to be in scale with what you can expect from that client on an ongoing basis, and with whether the client is likely to become a long-term client.

On the cost side, you can come up with an approximate figure for acquiring your average client by taking the total amount that you spend for marketing per year, and then dividing that figure by the number of clients you have acquired.

When considering whether to pursue a certain client, it is essential to be sure that you take into account the cost versus the value, as well as other factors such as the following:

- Does the client fits into the category of the one third of new acquaintances you like, versus the other two thirds (as discussed in a previous chapter). You must decipher whether the individual is your type of person, and if you will be comfortable working with them.
- Does the individual appear to be a potential lifetime client? Come up with an approximate determination of what this customer is worth to your business, both now and in the future.

Once a client has passed these tests and you have decided that the working relationship will benefit all involved, it is important that you then nurture your client investment going forward. Once the cost associated with acquiring a client is fully understood, it is much easier to see how clients are, in fact, highly valuable investments.

Properly Nurturing Your Customers Doesn't Cost—It Pays

There is certainly a cost associated with acquiring each of your clients. It is essential that you also allocate resources—both money and time—in nurturing your customer relationships, with the goal of long-term customer retention.

What will you do over the lifetime of your working relationship in order to keep the client yours? There are a number of key items that come into play here, including:

- support
- service
- account management

To truly set yourself apart from the competition, extra items should be involved so that you can stand out from the many other financial advisors a client could choose from.

How to Nurture Your Investment and Make It Grow

Getting clients and keeping them are, in many ways, completely different things. Not all customer retention strategies are equal, so you need to determine which will work the best for you.

A wise man once said, "There are basically two ways to generate more revenue for your business: Find more customers, or keep the customers you have and get them to buy more."[1]

Unfortunately, many financial advisors only implement the initial financial plan, and then get occupied elsewhere and neglect to address the client's other, ever-changing needs. This is definitely no way to become a trusted advisor. Every financial need of the client must be addressed consistently and over time if you wish to become a trusted advisor!

One of the top reasons why financial advisors lose clients is due to lack of communication with them. Client attrition can keep an advisor in the loop of continuously needing to go out and generate new business, rather than focusing on serving long-term clients and only getting new clients via referral.

Which way would you rather run your business: by comfortably and confidently obtaining a regular stream of referrals and repeat business, or by dialling for dollars for several hours every day?

You must consider your clients as investments that will reap rewards over time for you. To ensure that your clients remain with you for the long term, you must continuously nurture these investments.

There are several ways to invest in your clients:
- *Money*—How much revenue do you invest in customer success?
- *Time*—How much time do you set aside for analysing and creating customer satisfaction?
- *Culture*—What things do you do to celebrate your customers?[2]

According to Jeff Bezos, the founder of Amazon, "We see our customers as invited guests to a party, and we are the hosts. It's our job every day to make every important aspect of the customer experience a little bit better."[3]

Owning the Voice of Your Clients

One of the best ways that you can nurture your client investments is to "own the voice" of your clients. This starts with truly knowing your client, their goals, and the things that are important to them.

There are many ways in which you can essentially own the voice of your clients. These include some basic strategies, as well as doing a bit of thinking out of the box.
- Know and acknowledge the client's birthday, as well as the birthdays of their spouse and children.

- Send the client a welcome-aboard gift, as well as gifts on special occasions. Be sure that the gift goes to the client's place of business, not their home. That way, their co-workers and other business associates will notice the way you are nurturing your client, and they will possibly ask your client for your contact information.
- Know when the client's personal circumstances change and respond accordingly. For example send a card and flowers if a client has lost a loved one, or a suitable gift if they just had a baby.
- Connect with your clients on social media.
- Know what each client likes, such as their favourite coffee or snack, and keep it on hand to serve when the client comes to your office.
- Invite clients to appropriate events, such as the theatre or sporting events. For select client relationships, invitations to more intimate occasions, such as weddings, may also be appropriate.

Nurturing your clients can admittedly take time. During the initial stages of your client relationships, do not be surprised if your clients are a bit hesitant about giving you in-depth information about themselves, their interests, their goals, and their dreams. Strangers simply do not do this, so don't pressure them to open up right away. And do not get discouraged if they don't. When you are in the early stages of the relationship process, work to control your expectations, and the situation will become more manageable.

Eventually, given the proper amount of nurturing, a relationship will happen. In fact, when you nurture your investments, it is simply amazing how much more you will learn about them. Slowly but surely, you will play a much bigger role in your clients' lives as they build up trust in you. Because of this, you will be thought of more and more as a trusted advisor and also as a friend. Your clients will feel comfortable sending referrals your way, knowing that you will treat their friends and loved ones in such a nurturing manner.

Happy clients will continue to work with you and to refer other prospects to you. They will also do more business with you over time, as they truly see you as a trusted advisor—*their* trusted advisor.

Building Up Your Client Investment Account

Thinking of your clients as investments can help you make better decisions with regard to customer acquisition and retention, so as to generate both short- and long-term returns.

By nurturing your client investments like a farmer nurtures seed in the ground, client relationships will grow and prosper. The longer this goes on, the more sturdy the roots of your relationship will become. Warren Buffet sums it up best: "Someone is sitting in the shade today because someone planted a tree a long time ago."[4]

The Goose that Lays the Golden Eggs

There is one very important investment that we have not yet spoken about, and that is the goose that lays the golden eggs. That investment is you!

A few weeks ago, one of my long-time school friends lost two of his three restaurants due to things that were out of his control. The financial loss was, needless to say, quite substantial. He was absolutely distraught. He ended up in hospital with extreme hypertension, and his life was in danger.

I spoke to him and explained the concept that saved my life when, a few years ago, I was hit with a surprise and devastating divorce. I suffered substantial financial losses and, due to my emotional state, they were unfortunately ongoing losses.

Through it all, I reminded myself over and over again that I had only lost some of my golden eggs. I am still the goose and I need to protect the goose. I also saw my business as the goose, and the same rules applied to the business. I did everything possible to keep the goose alive, knowing that one day it would lay golden eggs again.

It is silly to neglect or possibly even to kill the goose just because some of the eggs have been lost. They are only eggs!

He quickly grasped the concept and got back on his feet. Within days, a new opportunity presented itself to him, and he now owns a lucrative butchery. Had my friend not taken that advice to heart, he may not have noticed when this new opportunity came knocking.

So often we pour everything we have into our businesses at the expense of ourselves—our health, our emotional well-being, and our private lives. But what is the point of achieving great success if we are not able to enjoy it and share it with others? Worse yet, what if our health fails and we die?

The well-known parable of the Mexican fisherman changed my approach to business forever. In case you haven't heard it, here is a paraphrase of it:

> An American investment banker was at the pier of a small coastal Mexican village when a small boat with just one fisherman docked. Inside the small boat were several large yellowfin tuna. The American complimented the Mexican on the quality of his fish and asked how long it took to catch them.
>
> The Mexican replied, "only a little while". The American then asked why didn't he stay out longer and catch more fish? The Mexican said he had enough to support his family's immediate needs. The American then asked, "But what do you do with the rest of your time?"
>
> The Mexican fisherman said, "I sleep late, fish a little, play with my children, take siestas with my wife, Maria, stroll into the village each evening where I sip wine, and play guitar with my amigos. I have a full and busy life."
>
> The American scoffed, "I am a Harvard MBA and could help you. You should spend more time fishing and with the proceeds, buy a bigger boat. With the proceeds from the bigger boat, you could buy several boats, eventually you would have a fleet of fishing boats. Instead of selling your catch to a middleman you would sell directly to the processor, eventually opening your own cannery. You would control the product, processing, and distribution.

You would need to leave this small coastal fishing village and move to Mexico City, then LA, and eventually New York City, from where you will run your expanding enterprise."

The Mexican fisherman asked, "But, how long will this all take?"

To which the American replied, "15 – 20 years."

"But what then?", asked the Mexican.

The American laughed and said, "That's the best part. When the time is right you would announce an IPO and sell your company stock to the public and become very rich, you would make millions!"

"Millions – then what?"

The American said, "Then you would retire. Move to a small coastal fishing village where you would sleep late, fish a little, play with your kids, take siestas with your wife, stroll to the village in the evenings where you could sip wine and play your guitar with your amigos."[5]

Success is not a destiny. It is a journey, a journey that is to be enjoyed and which is—or should be—secondary to living your life.

In our industry, we are privileged that we can structure our practices around our lives. It is all a matter of priorities. Years ago I adopted the following priorities:

- God and my spiritual life
- spouse
- children
- spiritual family
- work

I was mindful of protecting, caring for, and nurturing myself.

In my efforts to protect the goose, I carefully analysed my life and did my own toxic audit. I re-evaluated everything that I considered to be toxic in my life, including people, habits, possessions, mindsets, what I read, what I watch, and what I get involved with. This included anything that stole from me in some form or another. I eliminated as much as possible of it in order to see what effect it had on me and my ability to produce (lay eggs).

To aid in my divorce recovery, I went so far as to get rid of all my pre-divorce possessions, such as my clothes, house, and car. I moved to a new home and started over. I met a wonderful lady. Because of my hard work and commitment to recover from my divorce, we were able to start and maintain a healthy relationship. I am happy to say that we are now happily married.

On a daily basis, I eliminated negative people, news, and events as far as possible. I did regular exercises, changed my diet, and participated in hand-to-hand combat classes, tactical firearm training, and other activities I enjoyed—all while doing business.

Once the commitment is made to take care of the goose, then everything else can be structured around the goose. If you enjoy golf, then you need to find the time for golf. If you like massages and long walks on the beach, then take them and don't let yourself feel guilty about it.

One of my very best production months ever was next to a tropical lagoon in Mozambique. I worked for two hours a day and spent the rest of my time exploring the lagoon with my kids. It was one of the greatest months of my life.

Nurture the goose, because it is by far your biggest investment. Structure your life around the health (physical, emotional, and spiritual) of the goose and be ready for eggs by the dozens!

***

Success Action Steps

Clients are important assets in your financial services practice. It is important to carefully choose which customers you aim to work with, as well as to determine the cost of acquiring each client and the value that each brings to your business.

With that in mind, take some time and complete the following action steps:

1. How much does it cost you to acquire a client?

2. What is the value that each client brings to your business?

3. How does customer value drive your marketing strategies?

4. When you acquire a new client, what is the message you send to them? Do you welcome them as an individual with whom you want to build a long-term business relationship? Or does the client feel like you want to make a quick sale, earn a commission, and then move on?

5. What do you and/or your practice as a whole do to make the most of your customer relationships?

6. What can you implement immediately to protect and nurture the goose that lays the golden eggs? Remember, without you, the goose, there will be no business to serve your clients!

CHAPTER 8

JACK OF ALL TRADES, MASTER OF NONE

The jack-of-all-trades seldom is good at any. Concentrate all of your efforts on one definite chief aim.

—Napoleon Hill

All of my life, I have been a big fan of specialization. This started at an early age, when I learned how to fix VCRs. (For those who are too young to remember, video cassette recorders, or VCRs, were wired into the television set and were used for watching movies on large video tapes.) I worked for an electronics retailer for a time, and although the store offered televisions and other electronic devices, my sole focus was to repair VCRs. Because of my keen focus, I became quite good at it.

My knowledge and expertise in this area were so good, in fact, that I started my own business while I was a student at university. The money I made from repairing VCRs paid for my schooling, my pilot's license training, and of course the social aspects of my life, such as parties, girlfriends, and cars!

I later joined a national repair company. I was able to repair up to thirty-five VCRs per day, against a national average for VCR technicians of five to seven units per day. I became so acquainted with what were called "stock faults" (common faults on a given model of machines) that other repair companies started sending me their VCRs to repair. They paid my fee and added a mark-up to what they charged the customer.

Due to my extreme focus in the area of VCR repair, I would not have been considered a jack of all trades, nor a master of none. "Jack of all trades, master of none" is a figure of speech that refers to a person who has dabbled in many different skills, versus gaining expertise by focusing on one.[1] It may be nice to be a well-rounded person, but this does not help you stand out and differentiate yourself from the long list of other professionals that prospects can choose to work with.

The "jack of all trades" saying exists in many different languages. Though it has a similar meaning in every culture, it is interesting to note how people around the globe perceive it.

Some of these aphorisms include the following:

- Moroccan Arabic: "The one who knows seven trades but has no wealth."
- Syrian Arabic: "Who does several trades is incapable of managing any."
- Cantonese: "Equipped with knives all over, yet none is sharp."[2]

Breaking the Jack of All Trades Mould

In South Africa, financial advisors tend to offer a long list of products and services to their clients. This may be so that they don't leave money on the table, or so that clients will not leave them in order to purchase necessary products somewhere else. Other advisors are seen as potential threats, which sadly means that there is seldom collaboration between advisors. Ultimately, the one who comes up short is the client.

This is not the best way to go about building a successful practice. Displaying a huge list of products makes it extremely difficult to set yourself apart as an advisor. Your offerings seem more like a commodity than individualized and highly valuable advice for your clients.

Unless you make yourself visible to prospects, you run the risk of fading into the background with hundreds of other financial services professionals who have to hunt and peck each day to generate business. Some advisors work this way for their entire careers. It's not a very appealing way to spend forty or more working years.

One of the best ways to go about breaking the "jack of all trades" mould is to become a specialist and seek out clients and prospects who are part of a particular niche. In my case, this niche is pilots and other aviation professionals.

Specializing in a niche can have numerous benefits, both for the client and for the advisor. As an example, a few years ago I needed an indoor fireplace for my home. I phoned five installers and asked each one to come around and give me an estimate. They arrived at various times of the day, and I asked each more or less the same set of questions.

Four of the five contractors did general maintenance work, building and renovations, and other work. All four of these individuals quoted similar prices, and there was little that differentiated the estimates from one another, apart for a few small aesthetics.

The fifth quote, however, was completely different. In that quote, the installer explained that because I live right on the beach, I needed to consider some essential factors before moving forward with the job. These included:

- corrosion
- salt
- position of the chimney
- the Cape Doctor (a notorious south-easterly wind we get in Cape Town)
- occasional severe storms

He suggested a different site for the fireplace, as well as a different size and composition for the chimney. He explained in great detail why the changes were of the utmost importance. His estimate for this work was almost double the amount of the others. He was a specialist and only worked on indoor fireplaces.

I happily paid for his expertise, and he proved himself to be correct over and over. I have no doubt that if I had taken one of the other quotes in order to save money, I would have had to re-do all the work again by now, costing me much more in money and time.

This story clearly illustrates the immense value added to your proposition by specializing. The same holds true in a multitude of other industries. Take, for instance, the medical field. If you are having issues with your heart, you could get some of your questions answered by going to a general medical practitioner. But if you really want to know what is going on with your heart and what you can do to fix it, then going to a heart specialist is the only sensible choice. Getting your advice from a specialist will allow you to sleep much better at night.

Establishing Your Niche

The Merriam-Webster dictionary defines a niche as "A specialized market; A place, employment status, or activity for which a person or thing is best fitted." The most successful financial advisors will establish themselves in specific niches.

Your niche should be special. It must be unlike anything else that is available in the marketplace, even if you are offering the very same products that others are providing. Because your clients and prospects feel that you are talking directly to them about their needs, they will see you as the expert, the one who can help them solve their specific problems.

A niche can be in any number of areas.
- *Life Stage*: There are many areas of life stage that financial advisors can focus on. These include working with millennials, with small business owners, or with those who are post-retirement.
- *Industry*: Focusing on an industry is another way to differentiate yourself. For instance, my practice is focused solely on aviation professionals. I have studied literally every aspect of this industry, and am now considered a leading financial advisor in the world in this area. If a client mentions the type of airplane that they fly, I can provide them with an estimate of coverage rates and other key information that a generalist advisor would not be able to do.
- *Type of Planning*: Many successful financial advisors focus on a certain type of planning, such as estate planning. You could take this specialization a step further by offering estate planning specifically for small business owners, for example.

It is important to establish your niche early on in your career. Doing so will set you apart from the very beginning. Specialization allows you to more quickly and easily attain the clients that you most want to work with, and to eliminate those you don't. That is because you already speak the language of your potential clients, addressing their needs directly.

When you are a specialist, you can more easily get referrals from your clients. Your current clients are likely to know others who are in the same or similar positions, and who have the same or similar) needs. They will automatically refer these individuals to you. Each client in your niche helps to further build your business and is a stepping stone to your ultimate reputation.

This can cement your position in the industry. It can also help you to move away from having to make cold calls much earlier in the process of establishing your practice. (Personally, I have not made a cold call in many years.)

If you aren't quite sure how to choose a niche, it can be helpful to ask a series of specific questions:

- Is there a particular area that you are highly knowledgeable or passionate about?
- Are there any areas of the marketplace that are currently being underserved and where you could be of help?
- Are you a member of a particular niche?
- Is there any specific age bracket of people that you identify with or better relate to?
- Do you have experience in other industries that you could turn into your niche?

Mastering Your Trade for Success

As a master of your niche, you can offer your clients more value by providing them with specific information that directly ties into their problems and issues, as well as the solutions for these. So how do you become a specialist if you are not already one?

There are several ways to accomplish this. Start by taking a trip to your local library or book store, or to an online book retailer such as Amazon.com. By reading roughly twenty books on your topic or area of interest, you will become a specialist in that area. In fact, once you have done so, you will know more about your topic than 95 per cent of all other people in the world. Sounds ridiculous, I know, but it is really just that simple. It is said that generally after completing your entry-level training as a financial advisor, you already know more than 95 per cent of all people about financial planning.

Combining these two areas of expertise, you will be able to answer questions and address the concerns of your niche marketplace far better than a financial advisor who simply works as a generalist, making your advice and services that much more valuable even if the generalist offers more products.

In addition, if you are a fee-based advisor, you will also be able to charge more money for your services as a specialist than you would be able to charge as a generalist—in some cases much more, such as four or five times the going rate. And your clients will be happy to pay this price!

As you become more of a specialist, you could even consider writing your own book that provides readers more in-depth information. This can truly give you expert status in the minds of your clients and prospects.

Collaborating with Others Who Compliment Your Practice

Because trusted advisors have an area of specialization, they will not be able to solve all issues for a client. This, however, is not a negative thing.

Here is where you could partner with another advisor to assist your clients in other areas. This type of collaboration is seen by clients as being highly valuable. By collaborating with other advisors versus competing with them, you acquire a way of obtaining additional referrals.

You will be hard pressed to find a client who is unhappy with this concept if it is explained properly to them. I have only experienced positive feedback on this from my clients. I believe it shows them yet again that I am a trusted advisor and that I care about their portfolio more than my own pocket. Do not underestimate the power of this.

The Many Advantages of Specializing

According to the Merriam-Webster dictionary, the definition of a generalist is "a person who knows something about a lot of subjects." The definition of a specialist is "a person who has special knowledge and skill relating to a particular job, or area of study."

There are numerous benefits to being a specialist.

Client Acquisition: Being a specialist is extremely attractive to clients and prospects. When people work with you, they will feel they are getting advice that is pinpointed to their particular needs. This provides clients with peace of mind and can turn them into long-term clients. Acquiring clients can be much easier for a specialist than for generalists. Specializing can help you to stand out from the crowd. It can also be easier to generate referrals, as your current clients will want their colleagues to reap the same valuable benefits that they have. If you happen to have a slow period, you can pick up the phone and contact prospects in your specific niche, many of whom are likely to have heard of you through your networking efforts. This can create an instant bond and increase your chances of securing a meeting with them.

- *Expert Status*: Specializing can also put you at expert status in your field. Because of this, you may be sought out by journalists and / or media personnel to provide your opinion on certain situations that are related to your field. This exposure may then be seen by a multitude of potential clients, who will now see you as someone who can solve their specific needs.
- *Job and Income Security*: The longer you are a specialist, the more secure your practice—and, in turn, your income—will likely be. As a widely recognized expert in your field, people will tend to seek you out.
- *Higher Pay*: If you work in a fee-based financial services environment (versus being paid solely by commission), you will be able to charge more as a specialist. You may be able to earn the money you want while working fewer hours.

Moving Forward as a Master in Your Practice

Life can be filled with many distractions. While there is absolutely nothing wrong with an occasional diversion, you need to be very careful with how you spend your time and who you spend it with. Those who are able to make a real difference have mastered the discipline of focus.

Specialization can help you to build a credible and profitable practice. Mastering one specialty area does not necessarily rule out learning others, but having focus ratchets up your status as an expert in your given niche.

If you are going to be a master at something, you must forgo other avenues so that you can be truly great at your trade. In his book *The 50th Law*, Robert Greene writes. "Your goal is to reach the ultimate skill level - an intuitive feel for what must come next."[3]

Are you ready for what comes next?

***

Success Action Steps

Being a specialist can have far-reaching benefits for you and for your clients. If you have not yet chosen your niche, then do so now by considering the following questions:
- What specialized knowledge or expertise do I have?
- Are there certain types of people that I enjoy working with?
- Do my friends and colleagues say that I am particularly adept in a certain topic or field?
- Is there a certain industry that I am extremely interested in learning more about so as to achieve expert status?
- Are there any areas of the marketplace that appear to be underserved and where I can offer help to those who need it?

CHAPTER 9

JUDGE A BOOK BY ITS PROFILE

Communication - the human connection - is the key to personal and career success.

—Paul J. Meyer

How you communicate with your clients and prospects can tell them a lot about you and about whether they should trust you as their financial advisor. But communicating with others does not only involve what you physically say to them with your mouth—far from it.

There are several criteria by which a client or prospect may judge your worthiness to be their trusted advisor, and they can do so without you ever uttering a single word. These factors include your digital footprint, the micro messages that you project, and your personal congruency.

Your Digital Footprint

Up until a decade or so ago, if someone wanted to find out more about you, they had to make a conscious and time-consuming effort to find this information. That is not at all the case today.

Now your public profile is everywhere. All anyone has to do is turn on their computer or their smartphone and check a plethora of online sources, such as Google, Facebook, LinkedIn, or Twitter.

It may be fun to post pictures and statements online, but these may not always present you in the most positive manner, especially if you are building a practice whereby you aim to manage other people's money. Imagine if you were considering a financial advisor. Would you be apt to let someone manage your family's wealth if that person posted a steady stream of photos showing them drinking alcohol and partying? Or if they wrote endless political and religious rants?

Probably not!

Even if you are a highly educated and trained financial professional, if your digital footprint does not show you in a proper light, it can truly harm your ability to attract the clients you desire. Whether you like it or not, people will research you. No one will take you seriously if your online profile contradicts the image you portray professionally.

So, if you find yourself in a situation that would not show well on digital media, do all you legitimately can to keep it private. Nobody needs to see pictures of you dancing on the kitchen table in your girlfriend's underwear. When it comes to your digital footprint, be sure that you know where you've been, where you are, and where you're going. It is easy for other people, including your best prospects and clients, to find out.

Even if you personally don't post pictures or other items on social media, other people do! Make sure that you frequently google your name. If a client, prospect, or potential employer did that, what would they find?

Micro Messaging

While most of us communicate by speaking with others around us, the reality is that, even if you aren't saying a word, you could still be sending powerful messages to other people. One way of doing so is through micro messaging. What exactly are micro messages?

In the most basic sense, micro messages are the little things around you that either confirm or contradict what your voice is saying. As a trusted financial advisor who is vying to work with successful people, do you present yourself accordingly? Are your shoes clean or are they scuffed? Is your hair neat and combed, or is it dirty and unkempt? Do your socks match your pants and shirt, or are they each a different colour—with several holes? I know this is an extreme example, but you get the point!

Likewise, you will often find that a prospect wants to walk you out of their building at the end of a meeting. Will they find you driving a well-maintained, clean vehicle, or will they instead find a run-down and dirty car that has fast food wrappers strewn over the seats?

Even the smallest of items can communicate whether your spoken message is congruent with who you really are. It is easier than you might think to ensure personal congruency. In many cases, all it takes is looking in the mirror and asking yourself if you appear believable. Would you move forward with you as your financial advisor? Do you look professional, well groomed, and trustworthy?

If you don't have the resources yet to purchase a big-ticket item, like a vehicle, that is in line with your personal brand identity, then at the very least you can make sure that your vehicle is shining clean, inside and outside. If you happen to open the trunk in front of your client to put your briefcase in, then even the trunk must be neat and clean.

It is also extremely important that your micro messages do not turn into micro inequities. A micro inequity is a seemingly harmless message of devaluation. They are a subset of the estimated two to four thousand micro messages that individuals send each day.[1] Research has shown that in the space of just a one-minute conversation, an individual can send between forty and fifty micro messages. These small bits of meaning occupy a continuum from positive micro affirmations at one end to negative micro inequities at the other.[2]

Coined by MIT researcher Mary Rowe, PhD, the term *micro inequities* encompasses the following attributes:

- subtle slights that can devalue the other person
- imbalances of human actions
- indirect offenses[3]

Without you saying a word, the micro inequities you communicate can have a profound effect. That is because micro messages reveal your core feelings as well as your beliefs about yourself, your client or prospect, and the product or service that you are offering.

Certainly, micro messages can work to your advantage as well. When micro messages are filled with positive, affirming, and appreciative content, you accomplish two things:

- provide a compelling model of appreciation and respect for others to follow
- build trust and strengthen relationships[4]

Remember, micro messages communicate who you truly are. The micro messages you convey can let clients and prospects know that you are a serious individual—or, alternatively, that you are not.

So ask yourself this question: Does your micro messaging correspond with what you say and who you want to be? Nobody is perfect. We are all works in progress. Changing your micro messages to be in line with who you want to be is perfectly acceptable and even quite commendable.

Personal Congruency

Another way that humans communicate is through our personal congruency. This refers to the "matching up", or congruency, of what your mouth is saying and what your body is communicating. Another term for it is *body language*—the process of communicating non-verbally via conscious or unconscious gestures and movements. These include the following:

- facial expressions
- tone of voice
- eye movements and eye contact
- body position
- gestures
- demeanour
- attentiveness
- mannerisms

According to a University of California–Los Angeles (UCLA) professor emeritus of psychology, Albert Mehrabian, words only account for roughly 7 per cent of our communicated messages. The rest consist of non-verbal communication such as tone of voice and body language.[5]

These non-verbal elements are particularly important for communicating feelings and attitude, especially when they are inconsistent with your words (e.g., if your tone of voice contradicts the apparent meaning of your words). People will tend to believe the tonality and non-verbal behaviour, not the spoken words.[6]

Let's say you have your arms crossed over your chest when you are communicating with a prospect. This can indicate that you are being defensive. It can also project that you do not agree with the actions or opinions of the other person.[7]

Likewise, if you are biting your fingernails during a meeting, it can demonstrate that you lack confidence, that you are nervous, or that you are insecure. People will often bite their nails without even realizing it. Try to be aware of unconscious mannerisms like these.[8]

Your non-verbal communication may even be unintentionally rude or offensive. If, for example, you are tapping your fingers, that communicates that you are growing impatient.[9] This alone can turn off a prospect so much so that they will not follow up with you. Even your breathing can give away that you are nervous—and if you appear nervous, the person you are meeting with will most certainly pick up on it. They will be apt to think, "Why is this advisor so nervous? What are they not telling me? How can I believe this person?"

Not all body language is negative or inappropriate, though. In fact, there are some mannerisms that are considered very positive, and can help you to move forward as a trusted financial advisor. These include eye contact and affirmative movements. As an example, if you keep your head up and look at the person you're communicating with, it lets them know that you are truly interested in the conversation. You can show empathy by smiling or nodding your head.

You should always keep the palms of your hands upwards when talking to a client, as it is a sign of trust. Further, taking notes can let others know that you value what they are saying, and that you are highly engaged in the conversation with them.[10]

Your posture is also a key factor in your communication. Be sure that you maintain a relaxed posture, regardless of whether you're standing or sitting down. Keep your back straight but not too stiff. Allow your shoulders to relax. From time to time, lean slightly forward in order to hear the client better. This can reinforce the idea that you are comfortable with your surroundings.[11]

If you struggle with incorporating positive body language, then practice sales calls in front of the mirror or with somebody you trust. Ask them how they experience you and if they feel comfortable with you.

It is possible to fake body language, and positive signalling can be an acquired skill. However, that is against the concept of a trusted advisor. Trusted advisors don't have to fake anything.

One of the key components of how your body language behaves has to do with whether you truly believe in what you're saying and in what you're selling. For example, if you are selling insurance coverage to a prospect, but you don't really believe in the policy, your body will not agree with what your mouth is stating. In fact, if you don't truly believe it yourself, then your body will essentially say that to the prospect. Your prospect will receive the real message, and they will not likely move forward with the purchase.

So how can you get your body and your mouth to align with one another? The first way is to truly believe in what you sell. This includes believing in the value of what you are bringing to the client or prospect, also known as your value proposition.

When selling insurance coverage, then, you must believe in the following:

- the value of financial advice
- helping others and changing clients' lives for the better
- owning insurance coverage

One way to project this belief—and in turn to project congruency—is to own an insurance policy yourself. This shows belief in what you are offering, and it will help to prove this to the prospect.

If you do not believe in your products or services, then you should not offer them. You should move on to selling something that you do believe in. Otherwise, your body will just continue to tell the truth about how you feel, and your personal congruency will not flow.

Properly Communicating as a Trusted Advisor

Communicating with others spans far beyond what you say with your voice. The voice is just a small aspect of the overall communication process. How we communicate non-verbally can go a long way in determining whether prospects move forward with a sale or leave the meeting with the intent to never return.

How can you ensure that your non-verbal communication shows you in a positive manner? First, you need to present yourself properly. Never misbehave in public, as you never know who may see you. One foolish act can destroy your entire career. Good behaviour can help to attract the type of clients you want, and it can keep your personal congruency in check.

Next, make sure that you are sending the right type of micro messages, ones that are perceived positively by a prospect or client. You should be aware of what your gestures and mannerisms are really saying. Positive messaging will make you appear more confident and more believable as a trusted financial advisor.

Prospects today will look at all of the above factors—your digital footprint, your micro messages, and your personal congruency—to decide whether they are willing to trust you as their advisor. To be seen as a trusted advisor, your messages must match who you are and who you want to be.

Do yours?

***

Success Action Steps

Communication such as micro messaging can say much more about you and your ability to be a trusted advisor than spoken words can. With that in mind, take a personal inventory of all of the areas where you may be sending micro messages, and ensure that these messages match up with the way that you want to be perceived by clients.

These areas include the following:

- physical appearance (hair, clothing, watch)
- personal hygiene (cleanliness, smell)
- personal items (briefcase, vehicle)

Here is a fun challenge for you to take. Before your next big presentation do the following:

1. Have your vehicle thoroughly washed, inside and outside. Including the tires.
2. Cut your hair, beard, and nails so that you look neat and clean.
3. Buy yourself new clothes for the meeting—everything, even socks and underwear.
4. Use a new perfume or cologne.
5. Organize your sales material in neat folders and make sure it is printed in high-gloss colour.

Now see how you feel when you walk into the boardroom. You will feel like a million dollars, and your prospects will pick up on that.

Email me at andre@andreroos.com and tell me how the call went and if you got the deal!

CHAPTER 10

THE PROPHET OF DOOM

The sky is falling, the sky is falling!

—Chicken Little

If you attend any type of business or social event, or even if you are simply having a conversation with a loved one, you will find that people much prefer to talk about fun, positive, and upbeat topics, rather than the opposite. People often have a fear of discussing real but unpleasant issues such as death, disability, serious illness, and their own funeral arrangements.

As much as we don't want to think about it, these types of situations do occur. Because such issues can be financially devastating, they must be planned for ahead of time. Doing so can help to lessen the impact—at least financially.

The question is, which unpleasant incidents should we anticipate and plan for? The answer is any and all of them.

As a trusted advisor, it is your duty to not only bring up such topics with your clients, but to paint a vivid picture in their minds of what could happen if various scenarios were to occur. For example, what if a young father passes away? You need to dig down deep and paint a picture of how the surviving spouse and children would go on. Because people tend to shove these types of thoughts under the carpet, the scenario usually does not have a happy ending, at least not without advance planning in place.

Planning for the Unpredictable

Nobody has a crystal ball through which to predict the future, though life would be so much easier if we did. Because we do not know what the future holds, it is essential to plan ahead for all of the possible scenarios, regardless of how unpleasant they may be.

Therefore, a trusted advisor has to take on the role of the prophet of doom in order to discuss these "what ifs" with their clients. It is important to take clients down a path that they may not wish to travel.

When you're talking about these situations, it is essential that you are not afraid to momentarily take on the role of a prophet of doom. Be straightforward and honest with clients.

Doom-related scenarios can occur in numerous areas of one's life. They include death, disability, and a shortfall in finances for emergencies or retirement. Specific situations that are more common than one would like include the following:

- death of a spouse
- death of a parent
- death of a child or a grandchild
- diagnosis of a terminal illness
- funeral, cremation, and/or burial arrangements
- accident
- insufficient savings for retirement
- loss of employment
- incapacitation due to accident or illness

When you are meeting with clients to discuss these matters, it is important and sometimes even necessary to have the entire family present. This includes parents, grandparents, and possibly children, depending on their ages.

I will never forget my first death claim. My client, a helicopter pilot doing aerial firefighting, was temporarily stationed at a base on a farm a few miles out of town. I drove out to see him and his wife on the farm.

His wife had just given birth to their second daughter a few months earlier. She was tending to the baby most of the time while I was there. I went through the various risk scenarios pertaining to the husband. Because he was a pilot, we needed to deal with events that would cause him to lose his ability to fly, and thus incur loss of his income.

His focus was clearly on providing for his family. In fact, he was so serious about it that I almost forgot to deal with another very serious issue—what would happen to the family if he lost his wife or if she was incapacitated?

In South Africa, aerial firefighters work two main seasons, one in the north of the country and one in the south. This is due to the rainfall seasons being different. Each season is six months long, which means that most pilots are away from home for at least six months of the year.

For a father of two young daughters, the loss or incapacity of his wife would require him to stay close to home. Should he not be able to work away from home, he would effectively lose half of his income and be unemployed for half of the year. As a trusted advisor, it was my duty to point this out to him.

After we had done all the planning for the husband, I turned my attention to his wife and explained the risks associated with her. He was listening attentively, but she wanted to hear none of it. She was in fact rather agitated. But I pressed on because it was important, and because it was my professional duty to lead them down that path. I got the feeling that she was not impressed with me at all and wanted to get me out of there. Her attitude seemed to be, "How dare this man talk about my death?"

My proposal and duty were to do proper risk planning for the wife as well the husband. The cost to include his wife was minimal, and despite her obvious lack of interest, he proceeded with my proposal and added her to his risk policy. She was a mountain bike and cycling enthusiast and was performing very well in her sport. As she was in good health, she easily qualified for the insurance policy.

Five months after my meeting with this couple, I got a phone call early on a Monday morning. I always worry when clients call me that early. I answered, and the voice on the other end of the line said, *"Andre, ek het my vrou verloor!"* (Andre, I lost my wife!) While training for an upcoming race, riding a borrowed bike, she was hit by a distracted driver and died a few hours later in hospital.

Claims take top priority in my business. We sell trust, and we sell a promise. When there is a claim, it is our turn to make good on our promise and prove to our client and his loved ones that their trust was placed in the right place. I cleared my schedule immediately and flew up country to meet with my client. It was a very emotional meeting for both of us.

Fourteen days later, the claim was finalized and the life cover was fully paid. I met with the client again to put in place a new financial plan and update his portfolio, including investing the life cover proceeds.

To this day my client only flies the north season, close to his home. For the other six months, he supports himself and his daughters on the interest that he earns off the life insurance proceeds. Had I not dared to lead my client down a path that was uncomfortable, he would have lost half of his income or spent six months a year away from his two small daughters.

Understanding the Role of the Prophet of Doom

According to the Cambridge Dictionary, a prophet of doom is defined as "someone who always expects bad things to happen."

In the case of a trusted advisor, it is helpful if you first ask your client, "Do you mind if I take on the role of prophet of doom temporarily? In doing so, I will be leading you down a path that you don't want to go. However, it will be quite beneficial for you and your loved ones in the long run."

While a client may not be happy about the discussion, as was the case in my example, they will typically allow you to start it. Bringing up various scenarios can help the client to see more clearly the type of planning that should be done. They can also see just how bad things could be for the people they love and care about if the planning is *not* done.

The scenarios that you discuss when taking on the role of a prophet of doom should not only be the client's personal ones. It is imperative that you go over possible business related situations, such as:

- business succession planning
- buy and sell agreements
- death of a debtor

Serious financial damage can be done to a company and to those who rely upon it for income due to the death or disability of a partner or owner, the death or disability of a major debtor, an unexpected accident, or the impact of a natural disaster.

The following unfortunate events happened to a client of mine. His situation clearly illustrates the importance of dealing with business-related risks as well.

Let's call these the two businessmen in this scenario Dave and John.

Dave and John started an aviation company in 1994. Four years later, they entered into a buy and sell agreement and took out the life insurance policies on each other's lives. The agreement was updated a couple of times over the next ten years, but by 2004 it was mostly outdated.

In 2004, Dave left the business and was bought out by John. The business had fallen on hard times, and it was not able to carry two directors any more. Dave and John parted ways amicably and with no bad blood between them.

Unfortunately, none of their advisors at the time informed them about the need to cancel the buy and sell agreement, as well as the insurance policies related to it. So somehow, both Dave and John kept on paying for the policies.

Dave became my client in 2014. At our second meeting, I pointed out this problem to him and asked him to cancel the buy and sell agreement and the respective policies. Dave gave me assurances that he would deal with it immediately, but unfortunately he never followed through. I reminded him again in early 2016, and again he assured me that he would deal with it.

On 15 March 2017, John suffered a major heart attack and passed away. The buy and sell agreement was never cancelled, and so it took effect. Because of that, my client Dave became the 100 per cent lawful owner of a business that he had exited thirteen years prior. To make matters even worse for Dave, the business was in huge financial debt, and creditors were now knocking on his door.

At the time of me writing this, the problem has not been resolved yet. Financial sequestration is looking like the only option for Dave. Because of this, Dave could even lose his family home.

All of this happened because a simple agreement was entered into many years ago and was never cancelled when it was no longer needed.

There are thankfully many examples where proper financial planning not only saved the business and its employees, but also the livelihood of the loved ones of the directors.

Living Will

I often say to my advisors that our job is to avoid *secondary trauma*. The death or disability of a loved one is the primary trauma. Losing a home, car, or other valued belongings, or having to adapt to a drastic change of lifestyle is what I refer to as secondary trauma. While we cannot predict or avoid primary trauma, we can certainly plan ahead for secondary trauma. Doing so can make a situation quite a bit less traumatic, at least from a financial standpoint.

Having a loved one become incapacitated indefinitely is a catastrophic event that is often overlooked by insurance and financial advisors, even though it has huge secondary trauma attached to it. The client is still alive, so no life insurance cover will pay out. However, the client also cannot work and earn an income. They cannot sign any paperwork for a disability claim. Their money might be frozen in a bank account, though the bills of course are never frozen. In fact, due to an increased need for medical attention, the client's bills could become even higher. Loved ones are stuck between a rock and a hard place, unable to move on and unable to pay the doctors.

One effective way to plan for such an unfortunate event is to put a living will in place. A client can also give a spouse power of attorney, so that the spouse can act on his behalf if the client is incapacitated.

I do this type of planning often for my commercial pilot clients who fly in remote or war-torn countries. They are more likely to go missing, be captured, or crash. Again, this is definitely not something that any pilot likes to talk about, but still it must be dealt with. In such a case, a spouse (or other loved ones) can still make financial decisions via a living will or power of attorney.

Gambling

Opinions may vary when it comes to taking chances, but I believe most people believe gambling is not good. It typically only benefits the casino. According to the Oxford Dictionary, gambling by definition means "taking risky actions in the hope of a desired result". I think we are all well aware, though, that hope is never a viable strategy!

Gambling with your hard-earned money is like overtaking on a solid line in the road, without being able to see if there is oncoming traffic. You can only *hope* that there is not. And what if your entire family is in the car?

As crazy as it sounds, many people do this with their finances. The hope for a desired result is their only "strategy".

I often ask a husband in front of his family, "Mr Client, are you a gambler?"

Mr. Client, inevitably, responds, "No!"

Then I ask, "Why do you gamble with your family by not having proper life insurance in place?"

Most people think that they will be fine and that they will retire happily on a full income. To illustrate my point to my clients, I had a friend make me a roulette wheel. The wheel even spins. It works very well when talking about gambling.

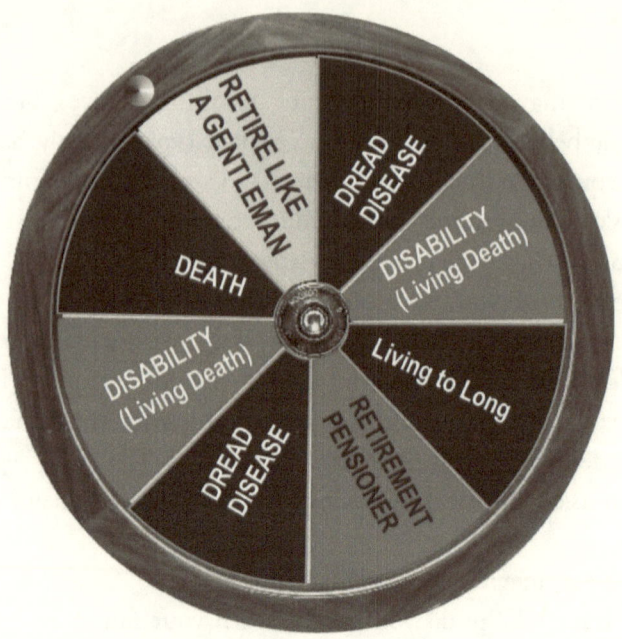

Go to www.andreroos.com to download this wheel in full colour.

Planning Ahead for the Unpredictable

Being successful in the risk management field requires that you ask and then help your clients answer a whole host of "what if" questions. For example, while it is not pleasant to discuss, you must ask very direct questions of them such as, "What if Dad passes away tomorrow? How will you deal with that? What would your lives look like going forward?"

According to author and president of the Institute of Internal Auditors, Richard F. Chambers, there are several key attributes of outstanding trusted advisors. These attributes are personal, relational, and professional.[2]

Personal attributes include the following:

- ethical resilience
- focus on results
- intellectual curiosity
- open-mindedness

Relational attributes include the following:

- dynamic communication
- insight
- inspirational leadership

Professional attributes include the following:

- critical thinking
- technical expertise[3]

As a trusted advisor, you cannot let your own fear of discussing these matters hold you back from doing so with your clients. If you do not bring them up, you are doing your clients a grave disservice. You *must* lead the client down these thought-provoking paths. You must also be as honest and realistic as possible with them.

And you can't stop after discussing one or two possible situations. It is imperative that you go over *every* potential scenario with them, just in case. You do not want the one scenario that you did not plan for to unfold.

What happens if the unpleasant scenarios that you and your client planned for never occur?

Actually, that would be great news!

But on the other end of the spectrum, if such events do happen, even just one of them, then your role as the prophet of doom will have been justified. By fulfilling that responsibility, the trusted advisor is able to help their client plan ahead and have the proper financial protections in place.

Becoming and remaining a trusted advisor involves not just what you know, such as risk and financial protection strategies, but also how you get things done with your clients. Both attributes are extremely important. It is only through their combination that one will truly become known as a trusted advisor.

Are you ready to take on the role of the prophet of doom in order to be your clients' trusted advisor?

***

Success Action Steps

As a trusted advisor, you must discuss each and every possible unpleasant scenario with your clients in order to best prepare them for the "just in case". There may be some situations that your client has not thought of, and they will be glad you brought up those situations, especially if one does unfold.

Take some time now to make a list of at least ten (10) different scenarios that you need to discuss with your clients. These should include both personal and business situations. Once you have done so, make another list of the possible solutions you could offer to your client for each scenario.

Possible Doom Issues
1. _____
2. _____
3. _____
4. _____
5. _____
6. _____
7. _____
8. _____
9. _____
10. _____

Possible Solutions
1. _____
2. _____
3. _____
4. _____
5. _____
6. _____
7. _____
8. _____
9. _____
10. _____

CHAPTER 11

TAMING THE FUTURE DRAGON

The future depends on what you do today.

—Mahatma Gandhi

There are few tragedies in the history of business that are more interesting than the demise of Kodak. In the early 1960s, this company, which had carved out a definitive niche in the world of film photography, employed approximately 75,000 people and earned more than $1 billion in US sales.[1]

So how could this large and powerful company now be nothing more than a memory?

Some might say that the answer is the competition. The reality is that the solution to Kodak's problems was actually well within the company's grasp for many years prior to its filing for bankruptcy in 2012.[2] In fact, digital photography, the technology that decimated Kodak in the 1990s and 2000s, was Kodak's own invention! However, the company's stubborn refusal to support the development that rivalled its core product, film, eventually brought Kodak down.[3]

Is your advisory practice at risk of going the way of Kodak? If so, it's time to start rolling with the changes.

The Only Real Constant Is Change

For billions of years, the earth has evolved and endured numerous changes. But at no time in our history has the communication landscape changed as quickly as it has since the advent of the Internet. This is particularly the case in the insurance and financial services arena.

Things like robo-advisors and other virtual solutions are becoming more common now, and paperless and virtual meetings are already a reality. New technologies are changing the operating landscape of the insurance industry. It is essential that advisors re-invent themselves in order to stay relevant and important to their clients. Advisors cannot get left behind.

Think about your life a decade or two ago, and then think about it today. How many of the everyday things that you focus on were invented in the 1990s or early 2000s?

- text messaging
- checking email from your phone
- talking to other individuals around the world "face-to-face" on your phone or computer screen (often at no cost)
- updating your social media profiles on LinkedIn and Facebook
- virtually sharing documents with someone in another location

These technologies can make our personal lives much easier and more convenient. Unfortunately, there are many advisors who are not tech savvy and thus not future-ready. This can be detrimental to their businesses.

Tools to Use for Keeping You Up to Date

There are literally millions of online and mobile tools available today that can simplify and speed up the processes of communicating with clients, gathering information, submitting paperwork, following up, and keeping in regular contact.

TimeTrade

Certainly, one of the keys to success in the insurance industry is having people to talk to. For most advisors, setting up appointments with prospects is the first step to what will hopefully become a long-lasting relationship.

One way to make this process easy and convenient is to use an online appointment scheduler like TimeTrade. Using this app, appointment times can easily be set up online, with times and dates filled in based on your real-time availability. You can reduce your risk of no-shows by sending customized email and text message reminders about the appointment. If a reschedule becomes necessary, that can also be done via this program.

Skype

In the past, insurance advisors served clients in their local area. This is because advisors needed to sit down and meet with the client in person, along with the client's spouse.

Today, though, it is possible that you may have clients who reside anywhere in the world. It is even possible that you may never meet some of your clients in person, yet still feel like you know them very well.

One way to meet and communicate with clients, regardless of where they are, is through Skype. Many years ago, chatting via video with someone who was half a world away seemed futuristic—something that only existed in science fiction movies. But now it is an everyday reality to sit down at your computer or smartphone and have a chat with anyone anywhere via the Internet.

Skype is currently the most popular "voice over Internet Protocol", or VoIP service. It is a peer-to-peer platform that allows users to make and receive video calls online. It is also free, which makes communicating easy and extremely cost-effective.

When using these technologies, it is often necessary to accommodate clients who reside in different time zones. Keep these demands in mind. You may need to set up Skype calls in the middle of the night or at other odd hours, based upon the time zone a client or prospect is in.

The ability to reach clients all around the globe, though, has literally opened up a world of opportunity. Gone are the days of working only in a local territory. There are no physical boundaries to contend with today.

GoToMeeting

Another popular service that you can use not only for communicating with clients and prospects, but also for sharing information on your computer screen, is GoToMeeting. This online desktop sharing and videoconferencing software enables users to meet with other computer users, clients, and colleagues in real time via the Internet.

This platform was designed to broadcast the desktop view of a host computer to a group of computers connected to the host. So with GoToMeeting, you can communicate with multiple users at once. For insurance and financial advisors, this can be particularly beneficial. It allows a real-time meeting between you, your client, and the client's other professional advisors such as their accountant and attorney.

Wufoo

If there is one constant in the insurance industry, it is paperwork. There is and likely always will be a plethora of forms to be completed. In many cases, you will be required to use the forms that are provided by the insurance carriers you're affiliated with. In other cases, you may be able to use forms that you have developed yourself. Doing so can be much easier if you use a platform like Wufoo.

Wufoo provides an easy form builder to customize and design forms. You can then embed the form directly onto your own website, so that it is easily downloadable for clients or prospects to complete and return to you.

In the past, a personal meeting was often required to gather all of the necessary information, which could be extremely time-consuming for everyone. By having helpful forms available online, clients and prospects can complete the information when it is convenient for them to do so. This often lead to gathering more complete information, which allows you to develop a better solution for their needs.

VMail

Keeping up with clients and prospects via email has long been a method of communication. But getting your message through can be difficult, as most people are stricken with email overload. With newer technology, there are ways to get your communication to stand out. One way is to send your messages through video email. This can be done via platforms such as VMail.

All you need is a webcam to record your message, and a video mail program that can store your video. Then you include a link in the body of your email so that the video can be played when the recipient clicks on it. You can also upload pre-recorded videos.

Expensify

Like all entrepreneurs and business owners, financial advisors must keep track of their expenses. Most good advisors are notorious for their bad admin skills. The fact is, though, lost receipts equal lost money. I for one have lost fortunes over the years simply because my record-keeping was dismal.

But the Expensify app saved my life. I simply take a picture of the receipt and the app "smart reads" it. The app even calculates the tax. The app files the receipt in my monthly report and automatically submits it to my accountant, complete with the photos, each month.

You can set up email forward rules on your fixed monthly expenses where you receive the invoices. This can easily be accomplished via email. Forward the emailed invoice to Expensify, and the system will smart read it and file it in your report. This app makes keeping track of expenses a breeze.

DocuSign

DocuSign enables people to electronically sign documents, approvals, and agreements on any device and in any time zone. In addition, this platform enables fully digital workflows that save money, increase efficiency, and move business forward.

Getting all of the necessary signatures on important documents used to take days or even weeks. This quick and easy platform can get all of your necessary approvals completed within hours. It allows you to send reminders and check the status of the document signing at any time. DocuSign provides a way to automate and streamline all of your business-critical workflows, saving time and money while remaining secure and compliant.

Customer Service and Claims Processing

The insurance companies themselves are also moving into the twenty-first century and are embracing technology, primarily by way of customer service, underwriting, and claims processing.

For example, in the past, when a policyholder needed to file a claim, they had to spend countless hours on the telephone, as well as additional time waiting for the paperwork to be processed.

Today, though, insureds can do virtually all of the necessary paperwork—well, virtually. And they can typically do so without ever having to talk with an agent.

Clients, Prospects, and Technology

It is important to keep in mind that, even if you aren't keeping up with the latest technologies, your prospects and clients likely are. Rest assured that they are running a Google search in order to research you before they decide to meet with you. When they do, what will they find?

It could be any number of things. For instance, do you have a nice website that clearly outlines how you help and provide value to your clients? Are there articles or white papers you have authored and posted online to educate readers?

Even if you are a highly educated and experienced advisor, your social media profile and other items about you that show up online may lead a prospect to believe otherwise. Therefore, while it is important to keep up with technology, be sure that you are going about it in the right manner.

Turning Change into Opportunity

Change can be difficult. This is especially the case if you have had a long-running and successful practice. In this case, you may think, "If it's not broken, don't fix it." One of the key points to learn from the story of Kodak, though, is that no one is ever too big to fail.

You cannot sit idle in the belief that business will continue as usual for years to come. You must be ready for the future. If you are still hauling around stacks of physical files or handing out business cards with no website address, then it may be time to re-evaluate your future readiness.

It is important to note, though, that while technology has ushered in numerous opportunities to streamline your business and to make it more convenient, people's ultimate needs have not necessarily changed over time. People still need to financially protect themselves and those they care about. This will continue to be the case well into the future. People want to know that they are dealing with an advisor they can trust, an advisor who is experienced and knowledgeable in providing the solutions they require.

It is still necessary to build a trusted relationship with your clients. Technology should serve the goal of letting them know that you have their best interest in mind, and that the products you're recommending are the ones that are the best suited for their specific needs and objectives.

In the words of Winston Churchill, "Success is not final, failure is not fatal: it is the courage to continue that counts."[4]

Are you and your practice prepared for the future?

***

Sales Action Step

Technology is changing the world at a rapid pace. Regardless of what business you are in, technological advancement is here to stay. Many of the apps and programs available today can make doing business easier and more convenient for advisors and clients alike. It just makes sense to implement technology into your practice.

Make a list of at least three apps or programs that you are currently not using, but that you should consider for making your business more streamlined. These may include some or all of the following:

- WordPress: website building and blog creation
- Skype: online phone calls and videoconferencing
- TimeTrade: online appointment scheduler
- GoToMeeting: online meeting and document sharing
- Wufoo: online custom forms provider
- VMail: video email messages
- Expensify: expenses tracking and accountant uploads
- DocuSign: electronic signature service

1. _____
2. _____
3. _____

CHAPTER 12

BARRIERS, BOUNDARIES, BALLS, AND WALLS

At its core, a fully functioning business is basically a set of systems and processes.

—John Jantsch, author of *Duct Tape Marketing*

While there are many sales methods that have been taught throughout the years, the reality is that in order to become a trusted advisor in any industry, you must provide your clients with value. In order to do that, it is essential that you earn trust, give advice effectively based on the client's specific situation, and build relationships.

This starts with having the proper mindset, which often requires that you rid yourself of old and outdated sales methods that you've been taught in training classes or by reading many of the traditional sales books.

Though it is still important to understand the psychology that drives people to make purchasing decisions, you do not have to engage in any kind of underhanded tactics or trickery in order to convince prospects to buy. Rather, by being honest about how they can protect themselves from the consequences of situations that they would rather not think about, you can secure your spot as their trusted advisor—and likely end up receiving more referrals from happy clients.

Andre Roos

Going Over, Around, and Through Barriers and Boundaries

Even on the most beautiful, clear day, storm clouds can pop up quickly and unexpectedly. This can make for a rough ride. Your success in the insurance industry can be difficult, too. Even among experienced, well-established agents, the occasional slump is not uncommon.

For example, clients and prospects often have instinctive barriers to buying certain products and services, particularly intangible items like insurance. They cannot immediately see the benefit, and in order to obtain the benefit, something bad must happen first.

Even the most polished, experienced, and successful insurance professional will hear no much more often than yes—no matter how much a client needs the product and regardless of how much the client trusts the advisor. In this industry, more so than many others, objections are a key part of the overall sales process.

However, based on the value that you provide to your clients, even on the toughest day (or week or month) can be well worthwhile in light of the ultimate rewards. This requires envisioning what you want your business to look like in the future, and then remaining steadfast on course to get there.

I always use the analogy of building a house to explain how our industry works. When you start out, you really only have a plot and an outside toilet. We call this the "long drop" in South Africa.

You start building your house. The first thing, of course, is that you need a plan. You have a huge pile of bricks to choose from. Some are brand-new and perfect. Others are used. Some are skewed, some are full of holes, and some are covered in dirt and old concrete.

If you are in a hurry, you can grab any brick and start laying the foundation of the house. A builder can be so eager to get out of a tent and into a home that they build with substandard bricks to get the house finished more quickly. But then the house leaks and takes endless hours to maintain. It's a house, but it is a nightmare to live in.

In the insurance agent analogy, the pile of bricks correlates to the pool of prospects available to the advisor. If you write policies for anybody and everybody you can get hold of, your book will be a nightmare to maintain and you will end up hating your job, and in fact your life.

I used to build my house like that, quickly and without a lot of thought, due to my desperate need to earn an income. Two years into my practice, my book of business was an absolute disaster. I had to break down the walls by re-intermediating clients to another advisor. Then I start all over again. I now have a properly built house that requires very little maintenance and is an absolute pleasure to live in.

Be sure to take your time, pick the perfect bricks, and lay them carefully. The rewards will be endless. That is the beauty of our industry: we can design our businesses and live the lives we want to live.

Ups never last; downs never last. We all have great months and bad months. Sometimes you have a great year, followed by a bad year. The secret is not to buy a Ferrari in your good year and not to commit suicide in your bad year. Business is a cycle that is often out of our control. Like a friend of mine says, "It is what it is."

Losing a Client

No matter how good you are, and regardless of how carefully you build your house, the reality is that you will lose clients from time to time. Again, it is a normal part of our lives. Even your very best client and golfing buddy might suddenly leave you without any explanation. How you respond to that client is what sets a trusted advisor apart from the rest.

I normally write a departing client a wonderful and respectful email, telling them I am sorry to see them go and wishing them all the best for the future. I offer my help in case anything is not well with his new advisor. Many times the client will continue to refer clients to me. Some even return to me later on.

Here is an email I received from one such client:

> Hi Andre,
>
> Hope all is well. Should have taken your advice regarding *****, scary the things they start to do. But so one learns.

> Would it be possible to get me a quote on life insurance, etc. please? Busy moving everything I have away from them slowly.
>
> Regards
>
> P—

Had I responded differently when P— left me, he would not have felt comfortable returning to me.

The simple rule is to always be the upstanding and honest trusted advisor no matter what happens. Stay true to your values, honour, and ethics.

Preparing to Take Flight

As you begin—or as you modify—your advisory business, it is important to ensure that you have all of the proper systems in place. Otherwise, you could go off course, and the earlier you veer, the more difficult it will be to steer back onto the right track.

With that in mind, be sure to review each of the action steps offered in each chapter. If any of them need to be completed or revised, now is the ideal time to do so.

These steps include the following:

_____ *Action Step 1*: Conduct an audit of your practice and remove everything that looks like sales from your marketing materials, including jargon.

_____ *Action Step 2*: Read through your list of clients and rate each one in terms of being relational or transactional. Take into account whether you really know the client and are familiar with the following factors about them. Answer each parameter with a yes or no.

You know the client's:

_____ spouse
_____ children
_____ parents
_____ friends
_____ goals (short- and long-term)
_____ hobbies
_____ favourite sports and teams
_____ attorney
_____ accountant
_____ doctor or medical advisor(s)
_____ spiritual advisor or mentor
_____ other advisors and professionals

The following additional factors should also be considered:

_____ You have been invited to the client's home.
_____ You have been invited to the client's place of business.
_____ You have been invited to special events in the client's life, such as holiday celebrations, weddings, or funerals.

Once you have completed this task with all of your clients, determine which ones you truly have a relational bond with, and which may be better served by another advisor.

_____ *Action Step 3*: Come up with a list of key questions to ask your clients. The questions should help narrow down their needs and to then come to an agreeable, collective solution to implement as a team.

_____ *Action Step 4*: Develop your formula or recipe for how you will spend your time each day in order to maximize your prospecting. This recipe should ideally be step-by-step actions that you can implement as soon as you reach your office each day.

_____ *Action Step 5*: Write down who your personal five professionals are.

1. Medical:_____
2. Tax/Accounting: _____
3. Legal:_____
4. Spiritual: _____
5. Financial:_____

Next, write down at least five points on how and why the fivepro concept provides so much value. This will help you to key in on certain points when explaining the concept to your clients and prospects.

1. _____
2. _____
3. _____
4. _____
5. _____

_____ *Action Step 6*: Consider how much it costs you to acquire your clients, as well as the ultimate value that each one brings to your overall business, now and in the future. Then answer the following questions:

1. How much does it cost you (in terms of money and time) to acquire a client?
2. What is the value that each client brings to your business?
3. How does customer valuation drive your marketing strategies?
4. When you acquire a new client, what is the message you send to them? Do you welcome them as an individual with whom you want to build a long-term business relationship? Or does the client feel like you only want to make a quick sale?
5. What do you or your advisory practice do to make the most of your customer relationships?

_____ *Action Step 7*: Being a specialist in a particular area or niche can have far-reaching benefits for you and your clients. If you have not yet chosen your niche, then do so now by considering the following questions:

- What specialized knowledge or expertise do I have?
- Are there certain types of people that I enjoy working with, such as retirees, business owners, or pilots?

- Do my friends and colleagues say that I am particularly adept in a certain area, topic, or field?
- Is there a certain industry that I am extremely interested in learning more about so as to achieve expert status?
- Are there any areas of the marketplace that appear to be underserved and in which I can excel?

_____ *Action Step 8*: Conduct a personal inventory of all of the areas where you may be sending micro messages. Ensure that these messages match up with the way you want to be perceived by clients.

These areas will include the following:

- physical appearance
- personal hygiene
- personal items

_____ *Action Step 9*: Make a list of at least ten different scenarios that you need to discuss with your clients. These should include both personal and business situations. Once you have done so, make another list of the possible solutions that you could offer to your clients for each scenario.

Possible Doom Issues

1. _____
2. _____
3. _____
4. _____
5. _____
6. _____
7. _____
8. _____
9. _____
10. _____

Possible Solutions
1. _____
2. _____
3. _____
4. _____
5. _____
6. _____
7. _____
8. _____
9. _____
10. _____

_____ *Action Step 10*: Make a list of at least three apps or programs that you are currently not using, but that you should consider for making your future business more streamlined.

1. _____
2. _____
3. _____

Make Sure that You're Always on Course

Becoming a trusted advisor takes work. Once you have built your practice to the level of success that you desire, it will still require that you regularly review your progress in order to determine whether you are still on course.

Given all of that, be sure that you review your practice, your actions, and your formula for success on a regular basis. If you are off course, this will provide you with a way to get back on course more quickly. Taking the time to do so will be well worth it for both you and your clients.

Building a trusted relationship with your clients will not only benefit them, it will benefit you too. Just some of the ways in which you can excel include the following:

- being seen as a trusted advisor, rather than simply a salesperson
- having clients accept and act on your advice, rather than having them leave your meetings to "think about it"
- having clients provide you with referrals
- earning a higher and more stable stream of income
- lowering the level of stress in your client interactions
- lowering the level of stress in your life overall
- being more confident and, in turn, more consistent

As an additional note, you should take some time to invest in attending a Million Dollar Round Table conference. I know it is pricey, but it will be the best investment that you can make in your future. There you will meet thousands of the top insurance producers in the world. It is a wealth of information and success stories. Spend time with advisors from many different countries and ask them how they became successful. I promise you that your life and business will never be the same.

My Personal Epiphany Moment

In conclusion, I would like to share with you a story that changed my life and career:

It was 3:30 p.m., and I had just finished a lengthy phone call with one of my clients, one who had become a dear friend to me as well. We joked about a few things and scheduled another appointment for the following Saturday. I had done a review of all his cover the previous Friday.

At 4 p.m., I received a phone call informing me that my client's helicopter had gone down. Fifteen minutes later, a second call informed that he had been killed in the crash. I broke down and cried right there in my office. It was a heart-breaking moment for me.

Early the next morning, I drove out to the town where he lived. It was about an hour's drive.

Besides giving my condolences to his wife, I needed her to sign a document so that his funeral benefit could be paid out.

When I arrived, there were, needless to say, many people already at her house: family, friends, aviation officials. Arriving just behind me was the family physician. I introduced myself to the others and explained that I just needed a few seconds with his wife, and I was happy to wait for as long as necessary. I understood that other things were more important. I found a couch and made myself comfortable, prepared to wait all day.

My client's wife was in her bedroom and the door was closed. As expected, the doctor first went in to see her. He came out a couple of seconds later and asked, "Who is Andre? She wants to see Andre."

This caught me a bit off guard, but I promptly stood up and made my way into her bedroom. I was thinking, *Why would she want to see me first?*

I greeted her, and before I could say anything more, she looked me straight in the eyes and said, "Andre, how am I going to live now?"

I said, "Judy, please don't worry about that. I did my job well. You and little Joshua (her son) will be financially taken care of for the rest of your lives."

That day I realized that being a financial advisor is not a job. It is not even a career. It is a calling!

NOTES

Chapter 1

1. Shutterstock https://www.shutterstock.com/download/success?u=http%3A%2F%2Fdownload.shutterstock.com%2Fgatekeeper%2FW3siZSI6MTUyNTkwMjc5NywiYyI6Il9waG90b19zZXNzaW9uX2lkIiwiZGMiOiJpZGxfNjY4NzgyMTE0Iiwiayl6InBob3RvLzY2ODc4MjExNC9odWdlLmpwZyIsIm0iOjEsImQiOiJzaHV0dGVyc3RvY3stbWVkaWEifSwielBUOUE3Y2daV1Z0d25QbmFjQnlFeU5ZU29JIl0%2Fshutterstock_668782114.jpg&pi=37925464&m=668782114&src=6AybAmImrOctO1WPrya7ZQ-1-5
2. "7 Old-School Sales Techniques You Must Avoid", HubSpot, https://blog.hubspot.com/sales/old-school-sales-techniques-avoid.

Chapter 2

1. "Roseto effect", Wikipedia, https://en.wikipedia.org/wiki/Roseto_effect.
2. Ibid.
3. Ibid.
4. John G. Bruhn and Steward Wolf, The Roseto Story: An Anatomy of Health (University of Oklahoma, 2003).
5. Ibid.
6. "Dunbar's Number and How Many True Financial Planning Client Relationships You Can Really Have", Nerd's Eye View at Kitces.com (October 10, 2012), https://www.kitces.com/blog/dunbars-number-and-how-many-true-financial-planning-client-relationships-you-can-really-have/.
7. Ibid.
8. "Why More is Less," by Barry Schwartz.

9. Ibid.

Chapter 3

1. "Daniel Pink Says That in Today's World We're All Salespeople," Forbes. https://www.forbes.com/sites/danschawbel/2013/01/03/daniel-pink-says-that-in-todays-world-were-all-salespeople/#736b22063818
2. "Caveat Emptor", Wikipedia, https://en.wikipedia.org/wiki/Caveat_emptor.
3. Daniel H. Pink, To Sell is Human: The Surprising Truth about Moving Others.

Chapter 4

1. "Sales Body Language", ChangingMinds.org, http://changingminds.org/disciplines/sales/articles/sales_body_language.htm.
2. Ibid.

Chapter 5

1. Saul McLeod Simply Psychology, updated ed. (2016), https://www.simplypsychology.org/maslow.html.
2. Ibid.
3. Hal Elrod, The Miracle Morning for Writers.
4. Ibid.
5. Ibid.
6. "Dress for Success," by Napoleon Hill.
7. https://www.goodreads.com/quotes/36-when-the-number-of-factors-coming-into-play-in-a

Chapter 6

1. Dawn to Dusk: An Essay on Humanity. By Dr. Shree Raman Dubey.

Chapter 7

1. Ty Kiisel, "4 Easy and Effective Ways to Invest in Your Customers" (23 Mar. 2017), https://www.helpscout.net/blog/investing-in-your-customers/.
2. "The ROI of Investing in Your Customers", Talkdesk (June 2, 2016), https://www.talkdesk.com/blog/roi-investing-customers-opentalk-2016.
3. https://www.brainyquote.com/quotes/jeff_bezos_173311
4. https://www.brainyquote.com/quotes/warren_buffett_409214
5. The Story of the Mexican Fisherman. By Courtney Carver. https://bemorewithless.com/the-story-of-the-mexican-fisherman/

Chapter 8

1. "Jack of All Trades, Master of None", Wikipedia, https://en.wikipedia.org/wiki/Jack_of_all_trades,_master_of_none.
2. Ibid.
3. "The 50th Law," by Robert Greene.

Chapter 9

1. Tom Larkin and Jean Marie Johnson, "Are Microinequities Damaging Your Workplace? Transform Them with Micro-MAGIC".
2. Ibid.
3. Ibid.
4. Ibid.
5. Albert Mehrabian Communication Studies. Institute of Judicial Studies. http://www.iojt-dc2013.org/~/media/Microsites/Files/IOJT/11042013-Albert-Mehrabian-Communication-Studies.ashx.
6. Ibid.
7. "Examples of Body Language", Your Dictionary, http://examples.yourdictionary.com/examples-of-body-language.html.
8. Ibid.
9. Ibid.
10. Kimberly Pendergrass, "10 Positive Body Language Techniques to Help You Succeed" 11 Dec. 2013), https://blog.udemy.com/positive-body-language/.

11. Ibid.

Chapter 10

2. Richard F. Chambers, "Trusted Advisors: Key Attributes of Outstanding Internal Auditors" (2017).
3. Ibid.

Chapter 11

1. Steve Brachmann, "The Rise and Fall of the Company that Invented Digital Cameras", IPWatchdog (1 Nov. 2014), http://www.ipwatchdog.com/2014/11/01/the-rise-and-fall-of-the-company-that-invented-digital-cameras/id=51953/.
2. Ibid.
3. Ibid.
4. https://www.brainyquote.com/quotes/winston_churchill_124653

www.ingramcontent.com/pod-product-compliance
Lightning Source LLC
Chambersburg PA
CBHW030805180526
45163CB00003B/1154